BEST-SELLING
1-STORY HOME PLANS

Contents

Getting Started

Maybe you can't wait to bang the first nail. Or you may be just as happy leaving town until the windows are cleaned. The extent of your involvement with the construction phase is up to you. Your time, interests, and abilities can help you decide how to get the project from lines on paper to reality. But building a house requires more than putting pieces together. Whoever is in charge of the process must competently manage people as well as supplies, materials, and construction. He or she will have to

- Make a project schedule to plan the orderly progress of the work. This can be a bar chart that shows the time period of activity by each trade.
- Establish a budget for each category of work, such as foundation, framing, and finish carpentry.
- Arrange for a source of construction financing.
- Get a building permit and post it conspicuously at the construction site.
- Line up supply sources and order materials.
- Find subcontractors and negotiate their contracts.
- Coordinate the work so that it progresses smoothly with the fewest conflicts.
- Notify inspectors at the appropriate milestones.
- Make payments to suppliers and subcontractors.

You as the Builder

You'll have to take care of every logistical detail yourself if you decide to act as your own builder or general contractor. But along with the responsibilities of managing the project, you gain the flexibility to do as much of your own work as you want and subcontract out the rest. Before taking this path, however, be sure you have the time and capabilities. Do you also have

the time and ability to schedule the work, hire and coordinate subs, order materials, and keep ahead of the accounting required to manage the project successfully? If you do, you stand to save the amount that a general contractor would charge to take on these responsibilities, normally 15 to 30 percent of the construction cost. If you take this responsibility on but mismanage the project, the potential savings will erode and may even cost you more than if you had hired a builder in the first place. A subcontractor might charge extra for

Acting as the builder, above, requires the ability to hire and manage subcontractors.

Building a home, opposite, includes the need to schedule building inspections at the appropriate milestones.

having to return to the site to complete work that was originally scheduled for an earlier date. Or perhaps because you didn't order the windows at the beginning, you now have to pay for a recent cost increase. (If you had hired a builder in the first place he or she would absorb the increase.)

Hiring a Builder to Handle Construction

A builder or general contractor will manage every aspect of the construction process. Your role after signing the construction contract will be to make regular progress payments and ensure that the work for which you are paying has been completed. You will also consult with the builder and agree to any changes that may have to be made along the way.

Leads for finding builders might come from friends or neighbors who have had contractors build, remodel, or add to their homes. Real-estate agents and bankers may have some names handy but are more likely familiar with the builder's ability to complete projects on time and budget than the quality of the work itself.

The next step is to narrow your list of candidates to three or four who you think can do a quality job and work harmoniously with you. Phone each builder to see whether he or she is interested in being considered for your project. If so, invite the builder to an interview at your home. The meeting will serve two purposes. You'll be able to ask the candidate about his or her experience, and you'll be able to see whether or not your personalities are compatible. Go over the plans with the builder to make certain that he or she understands the scope of the project. Ask if they have constructed similar houses. Get references, and check the builder's standing with the Better Business Bureau. Develop a short list of builders, say three, and ask them to submit bids for the project.

Contracts

Lump-Sum Contracts

A lump-sum, or fixed-fee, contract lets you know from the beginning just what the project will cost, barring any changes made because of your requests or unforeseen conditions. This form works well for projects that promise few surprises and are well defined from the outset by a complete set of contract documents. You can enter into a fixed-price contract by negotiating with a single builder on your short list or by obtaining bids from three or four builders. If you go the latter route, give each bidder a set of documents and allow at least two weeks for them to submit their bids. When you get the bids, decide who you want and call the others to thank them for their efforts. You don't have to accept the lowest bid, but it probably makes sense to do so since you have already honed the list to builders you trust. Inform this builder of your intentions to finalize a contract.

Cost-Plus-Fee Contracts

Under a cost-plus-fee contract, you agree to pay the builder for the costs of labor and materials, as verified by receipts, plus a fee that represents the builder's overhead and profit. This arrangement is sometimes referred to as "time and materials." The fee can range between 15 and 30 percent of the incurred costs. Because you ultimately pick up the tab — whatever the costs — the contractor is never at risk, as he is with a lump-sum contract. You won't know the final total cost of a cost-plus-fee contract until the project is built and paid for. If you can live with that uncertainty, there are offsetting advantages. First, this form allows you to accommodate unknown conditions much more easily than does a lump-sum contract. And rather than being tied down by the project documents, you will be free to make changes at any point along the way. This can be a trap, though. Watching the project take shape will spark the desire to add something or do something differently. Each change costs more, and the accumulation can easily exceed your budget. Because of the uncertainty of the final tab and the built-in advantage to the contractor, you should think twice before entering into this form of contract.

Contract Content

The conditions of your agreement should be spelled out thoroughly in writing and signed by both parties, whatever contractual arrangement you make with your builder. Your contract should include provisions for the following:

- The names and addresses of the owner and builder.
- A description of the work to be included ("As described in the plans and specifications dated . . .").
- The date that the work will be completed if time is of the essence.
- The contract price for lump-sum contracts and the builder's allowed profit and overhead costs for changes.
- The builder's fee for cost-plus-fee contracts and the method of accounting and requesting payment.
- The criteria for progress payments (monthly, by project milestones) and the conditions of final payment.
- A list of each drawing and specification section that is to be included as part of the contract.
- Requirements for guarantees. (One year is the standard period for which contractors guarantee the entire project, but you may require specific guarantees

When submitting bids, all of the builders should base their estimates on the same specifications. Once the work begins, communicate with your builder to keep the work proceeding smoothly.

Inspect your newly built home, if possible, before the builder closes it up and finishes it.

on certain parts of the project, such as a 20-year guarantee on the roofing.)

■ Provisions for insurance.

■ A description of how changes in the work orders will be handled.

The builder may have a standard contract that you can tailor to the specifics of your project. These contain complete specific conditions with blanks that you can fill in to fit your project and a set of "general conditions" that cover a host of issues from insurance to termination provisions. It's always a good idea to have an attorney review the draft of your completed contract before signing it.

Working with Your Builder

The construction phase officially begins when you have a signed copy of the contract and copies of any insurance required from the builder. It's not unheard of for a builder to request an initial payment of 10 to 20 percent of the total cost to cover mobilization costs, those costs associated with obtaining permits and getting set up to begin the actual construction. If you agree to this, keep a careful eye on the progress of the work to ensure that the total paid out at any one time doesn't get too far out of sync with the actual work completed.

What about changes? From here on, it's up to you and your builder to proceed in good faith and to keep the channels of communication open. Even so, changes of one sort or another beset every project, and they usually add to its cost.

Light at the End of the Tunnel.

The builder's request for a final inspection marks the end of the construction phase — almost. At the final inspection meeting, you and the builder will inspect the work, noting any defects or incomplete items on a "punch list." When the builder tidies up the punch list items, you should reinspect. Sometimes, builders go on to another job and take forever to clean up the last few details, so only after all items on the list have been completed satisfactorily should you release the final payment, which often accounts for the builder's profit.

Some Final Words

Having a positive attitude is important when undertaking a project as large as building a home. A positive attitude can help you ride out the rigors and stress of the construction process.

Stay Flexible. Expect problems, because they certainly will occur. Weather can upset the schedule you have established for subcontractors. A supplier may get behind on deliveries, which also affects the schedule. An unexpected pipe may surprise you during excavation. Just as certain, every problem that comes along has a solution if you are open to it.

Be Patient. The extra days it may take to resolve a construction problem will be forgotten once the project is completed.

Express Yourself. If what you see isn't exactly what you thought you were getting, don't be afraid to look into changing it. Or you may spot an unforeseen opportunity for an improvement. Changes usually cost more money, though, so don't make frivolous decisions.

Finally, watching your home go up is exciting, so stay upbeat. Get away from your project from time to time. Dine out. Take time to relax. A positive attitude will make for smoother relations with your builder. An optimistic outlook will yield better-quality work if you are doing your own construction. And though the project might seem endless while it is under way, keep in mind that all the planning and construction will fade to a faint memory at some time in the future, and you will be getting a lifetime of pleasure from a home that is just right for you.

Images provided by designer/architect.

CAD FILE AVAILABLE

Plan #F01-761005

Dimensions: 37'6" W x 52' D

Levels: 1

Heated Square Footage: 1,281

Bedrooms: 3

Bathrooms: 2

Foundation: Basement

Materials List Available: Yes

Price Category: B

This small home is packed with big style thanks to a wide open floor plan just like homeowners want today.

Features:

• Dining Room: The dining room offers a covered rear porch, which is the perfect size for a barbecue grill.

• Great Room: The great room has an 11' ceiling, a fireplace for warmth, and easy access to the dining area.

• Kitchen: The well-appointed kitchen enjoys an angled, raised counter perfect for casual dining.

• Master Bedroom: The vaulted master bedroom enjoys a sizeable walk-in closet and its own private bath.

MBr
12-9x14-3
Vaulted

Br 2
10-4x10-2

Porch

Dn

Br 3
10-4x10-0

P

Dining
10-2x10-8

Kitchen
10-6x10-8

L

DW   R

Great Rm
15-2x16-0
11' Clg

Garage
19-4x20-4

E

Porch

Copyright by designer/architect.

Plan #F01-191030

Dimensions: 33' W x 36' D

Levels: 1

Heated Square Footage: 864

Bedrooms: 2

Bathrooms: 1

Foundation: Crawl space or slab

Materials List Available: No

Price Category: C

Enjoy the view from the spacious front porch of this cozy cottage, which is ideal for a retirement home, vacation retreat, or starter home.

Features:

- **Porch:** This 6-ft.-wide porch, which runs the length of the home, gives you plenty of space to set up a couple of rockers next to a potted herb garden.

- **Living/Dining Room:** This huge living and dining area gives you many options for design. The snack bar that it shares with the kitchen is a practical touch.

- **Kitchen:** The first thing you'll notice in this well-planned kitchen is how much counter and storage space it offers.

- **Laundry Room:** Opening to the backyard, this room also features ample storage space.

- **Bedrooms:** Both rooms have good closet space and easy access to the large, luxurious bath.

Copyright by designer/architect.

LAUNDRY
12'-0" X 6'-0"

BEDROOM 2
13'-0" x 10'-0"

KITCHEN
11'-10"x9'-10"

snack bar

HVAC

BEDROOM 1
13'-0" x 10'-0"

LIVING/DINING ROOM
20'-0"X 14'-0"

6' WIDE COVERED PORCH

36'-0"

33'-0"

Plan #F01-181216

Dimensions: 31'8" W x 30' D

Levels: 1

Heated Square Footage: 910

Bedrooms: 2

Bathrooms: 1

Foundation: Basement; crawl space or slab for fee

Materials List Available: Yes

Price Category: B

CAD FILE AVAILABLE • CAD

A lot of creativity goes into creating this comfortable home. It begins with a Creole-style covered front porch that lines up across the entire front of the house, beckoning folks to relax awhile in the cool summer shade.

Features:

- Front Door: This entry door has something special - transom and sidelight windows to brighten the interior with natural light.

- Family Room: This large and open room eases to other important rooms - including the great-sized kitchen.

- Kitchen: This large eat-in kitchen has hearty cabinet and counter space.

- Bedrooms: A roomy full bathroom pampers two full-sized bedrooms, which are enhanced by unusual windows and excellent closet space.

12'-0" X 11'-0"
3,60 X 3,30

15'-8" X 11'-0"
4,70 X 3,30

30'-0"
9,0 m

10'-0" X 9'-0"
3,00 X 2,70

15'-8" X 13'-4"
4,70 X 4,00

31'-8"
9,5 m

Plan #F01-341146

Dimensions: 40' W x 29'4" D

Levels: 1

Heated Square Footage: 960

Bedrooms: 3

Bathrooms: 2

Foundation: Crawl space; basement or slab for fee

Materials List Available: No

Price Category: A

Images provided by designer/architect.

Copyright by designer/architect.

Plan #F01-341026

Dimensions: 39'9" W x 26' D

Levels: 1

Heated Square Footage: 1,009

Bedrooms: 3

Bathrooms: 2

Foundation: Crawl space; slab or basement for fee

Materials List Available: Yes

Price Category: B

Images provided by designer/architect.

Copyright by designer/architect.

Rear Elevation

Plan #F01-401047

Dimensions: 38' W x 34' D

Levels: 1

Heated Square Footage: 1,064

Bedrooms: 2

Bathrooms: 1

Foundation: Crawl space or basement

Materials List Available: Yes

Price Category: B

Images provided by designer/architect.

CAD FILE AVAILABLE — CAD

Copyright by designer/architect.

Rear View

Plan #F01-181345

Dimensions: 34' W x 34' D

Levels: 1

Heated Square Footage: 1,079

Bedrooms: 2

Bathrooms: 1

Foundation: Basement; crawl space or slab for fee

Materials List Available: Yes

Price Category: D

Images provided by designer/architect.

CAD FILE AVAILABLE — CAD

13'-0"x 22'-8"
3,90 x 6,80

12'-8"x 10'-4"
3,80 x 3,10

9'-0"x 10'-0"
2,70 x 3,00

12'-0"x 9'-4"
3,60 x 2,80

12'-0"x 12'-4"
3,60 x 3,70

34'-0"
10,2 m

36'-0"
10,8 m

Plan #F01-181148

Dimensions: 36' W x 34' D

Levels: 1

Heated Square Footage: 1,174

Bedrooms: 3

Bathrooms: 1

Foundation: Basement; crawl space or slab for fcc

Materials List Available: Yes

Price Category: E

Images provided by designer/architect.

CAD FILE AVAILABLE

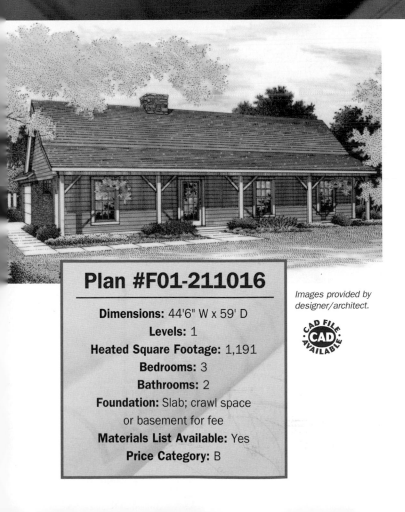

Plan #F01-211016

Dimensions: 44'6" W x 59' D

Levels: 1

Heated Square Footage: 1,191

Bedrooms: 3

Bathrooms: 2

Foundation: Slab; crawl space or basement for fee

Materials List Available: Yes

Price Category: B

Images provided by designer/architect.

CAD FILE AVAILABLE

garage 22 x 21

patio

sto 11x5

util 11x5

dining 12 x 12

br 3 12 x 10

kit 12x10

mbr 16 x 12

living 18 x 16

br 2 12 x 10

porch 42 x 5

Plan #F01-341004

Dimensions: 56'10" W x 28'6" D
Levels: 1
Heated Square Footage: 1,101
Bedrooms: 3
Bathrooms: 2
Foundation: Crawl space; slab or basement for fee
Materials List Available: Yes
Price Category: C

You'll love the romantic feeling that the gables and front porch give to this well designed home, with its family-oriented layout.

Features:

- Living Room: The open design between this spacious room and the kitchen/dining area makes this home as ideal for family activities as it is for entertaining.

- Outdoor Living Space: A French door opens to the back deck, where you're sure to host alfresco dinners or easy summer brunches.

- Kitchen: Designed for the cook's convenience, this kitchen features ample work area as well as excellent storage space in the nearby pantry.

- Laundry Area: Located behind closed doors to shut out the noise, this laundry closet is conveniently placed.

- Master Suite: With triple windows, a wide closet, and a private bath, this is a luxurious suite.

Images provided by designer/architect.

SMARTtip

Creating Depth with Wall Frames

Wall frames create an illusion of depth and density because
1) they are three-dimensional and
2) they divide the wall area into smaller, denser segments.

The three-dimensional quality of wall frames is fundamentally different from that of the alternative treatment: raised panels. Despite the name, raised panels actually produce a concave-like, or receding, effect whereas wall frames are more convex, protruding outward. In terms of sculpture, concave units create negative space while convex units create positive space. Raised panels, therefore, deliver a uniform sense of volume, mass, and density, while wall frames create a higher level of tension and dramatic interest.

Copyright by designer/architect.

Images provided by designer/architect.

Plan #F01-181021

Dimensions: 37' W x 44' D

Levels: 1

Heated Square Footage: 1,124

Bedrooms: 2

Bathrooms: 1

Foundation: Basement; crawl space or slab for fee

Materials List Available: Yes

Price Category: E

This cozy country cottage is enhanced by lattice trim details over the porch and garage.

Features:

- Ceiling Height: 8 ft.

- Living Room: This living room gets extra architectural interest from a sunken floor. This room, located directly to the left of the entry hall, has plenty of space for entertaining.

- Dining Room: This dining room is located in center of the home. It's adjacent to the kitchen to make it easy to serve meals.

- Kitchen: This bright and efficient kitchen is a real pleasure in which to work. It includes a pantry and double sinks. There's a breakfast bar that will see plenty of informal meals for families on the go.

- Covered Porch: This is the perfect place in which to retire after dinner on a warm summer evening.

- Bedrooms: Each of the two bedrooms has its own closet. They share a full bathroom.

Copyright by designer/architect.

Images provided by designer/architect.

Plan #F01-121144

Dimensions: 40' W x 48'8" D

Levels: 1

Heated Square Footage: 1,195

Bedrooms: 3

Bathrooms: 2

Foundation: Basement; crawl space or slab for fee

Materials List Available: Yes

Price Category: B

This is the right design if you want a home that will be easy to expand as your family grows.

Features:

- **Front Porch:** Hang baskets of plants from the roof of this porch, which is just the right size for a couple of comfortable rocking chairs and a side table.

- **Family Room:** This family room welcomes you as you enter the home. A crackling fire enhances the ambiance of the room.

- **Kitchen:** This intelligently designed kitchen has an efficient U-shape layout. A serving bar open to the dining area is a feature that makes entertaining easier.

- **Master Suite:** This is a compact space that is designed to feel large, and it includes a walk-in closet. The master bath is an added bonus.

Plan #F01-401020

Dimensions: 55'6" W x 30' D

Levels: 1

Heated Square Footage: 1,230

Bedrooms: 3

Bathrooms: 2

Foundation: Crawl space or basement

Materials List Available: Yes

Price Category: B

This is a grand vacation or retirement home, designed for views and the outdoor lifestyle. The full-width deck complements the abundant windows in the rooms that face it.

Features:

• Living Room: This area, with a vaulted ceiling, a fireplace, and full-height windows overlooking the deck, is made for gathering.

• Dining Room: This room is open to the living room; it has sliding glass doors that lead to the outdoors.

• Kitchen: This room has a pass-through counter to the dining room and is U-shaped in design.

• Bedrooms: Two family bedrooms in the middle of the plan share a full bath.

• Master Suite: This area has a private bath and deck views.

Images provided by designer/architect.

CAD FILE AVAILABLE

55'6 (16.9m)

30' (9.1 m)

br2 9'2"x10'4"

br3 9'2"x10'4"

mbr 13'2"x11'4"

liv 21'x15' VAULTED

k 10' x 11'8"

din 10'x11'4"

W D H

WS

Copyright by designer/architect.

DECK

Left Elevation

Rear Elevation

Right Elevation

rough in bath

unfinished basement

up

Optional Basement Level

Plan #F01-181714

Dimensions: 38' W x 36'4" D

Levels: 1

Heated Square Footage: 1,244

Bedrooms: 2

Bathrooms: 1

Foundation: Basement; crawl space or slab for fee

Materials List Available: Yes

Price Category: E

Images provided by designer/architect.

CAD FILE CAD AVAILABLE

12'-6" X 12'-2"
3,75 X 3,65

17'-4" X 15'-0"
5,20 X 4,50

13'-4" X 16'-0"
4,00 X 4,80

11'-0" X 10'-0"
3,30 X 3,00

Copyright by designer/architect.

Plan #F01-341304

Dimensions: 40' W x 41'4" D

Levels: 1

Heated Square Footage: 1,248

Bedrooms: 4

Bathrooms: 2

Foundation: Crawl space; basement or slab for fee

Materials List Available: Yes

Price Category: C

Images provided by designer/architect.

40'-0"

41'-4"

STORAGE

STOOP

BEDROOM 1
12'-8" X 9'-6"

BATH 1

KITCHEN & DINING
17'-6" X 9'-6"

CLOSET

CLOSET

LIN.

CLOSET

BEDROOM 2
10'-8" X 10'-0"

BATH 2

LIVING ROOM
15'-8" X 13'-6"

CLOSET

BEDROOM 3
10'-8" X 11'-6"

CLOS

BEDROOM 4
9'-8" X 11'-6"

PORCH

Copyright by designer/architect.

Plan #F01-131008

Dimensions: 45'4" W x 36'4" D

Levels: 1

Heated Square Footage: 1,299

Bedrooms: 3

Bathrooms: 2

Foundation: Crawl space; basement for fee

Materials List Available: Yes

Price Category: C

Images provided by designer/architect.

Rear View

Plan #F01-371093

Dimensions: 50' W x 45' D

Levels: 1

Heated Square Footage: 1,300

Bedrooms: 3

Bathrooms: 2

Foundation: Crawl space, slab, or basement

Materials List Available: No

Price Category: B

Images provided by designer/architect.

Optional Basement Level

Plan #F01-341028

Dimensions: 40' W x 32' D

Levels: 1

Heated Square Footage: 1,248

Bedrooms: 3

Bathrooms: 2

Foundation: Crawl space; slab or basement for fee

Materials List Available: Yes

Price Category: C

Images provided by designer/architect.

This home's efficient layout and comfortable living spaces all add up to a charming design that is perfect for many first-time homebuyers.

Features:

- Living Room: This spacious living room features a fireplace and twin windows.

- Kitchen/Dining Room: This kitchen/dining room provides a pantry and convenient access to the deck at the back of the home.

- Master Suite: You will love this master suite's dual-sink vanity and spacious walk-in closet.

- Utility Room: A separate utility room reduces the noise created by the washer and dryer.

Plan #F01-251001

Dimensions: 61'3" W x 40'6" D

Levels: 1

Heated Square Footage: 1,253

Bedrooms: 3

Bathrooms: 2

Foundation: Crawl space or slab

Materials List Available: Yes

Price Category: B

Images provided by designer/architect.

- Master Bedroom: This master bedroom features a large walk-in closet. It has its own master bath with a single vanity, a tub, and a walk-in shower.

- Garage: This attached garage provides plenty of extra storage space, as well as parking for two cars.

This charming country home has a classic full front porch for enjoying summertime breezes.

Features:

- Ceiling Height: 8 ft.

- Foyer: Guests will walk through the covered front porch into this foyer, which opens to the family room.

- Rear Porch: A second porch is covered and is located at the rear of the home off of the dining room, so your guests can step out for a bit of fresh air after dinner.

- Family Room: Family and friends will be drawn to this large open space, with its handsome fireplace and sloped ceiling.

- Kitchen: This open and airy kitchen is a pleasure in which to work. It has ample counter space and a pantry.

Plan #F01-321033

Dimensions: 38' W x 46' D
Levels: 1
Heated Square Footage: 1,268
Bedrooms: 3
Bathrooms: 2
Foundation: Basement or slab
Materials List Available: Yes
Price Category: D

Images provided by designer/architect.

- **Master Suite:** Everyone knows that the master bath makes the master suite, and this home is no different. His and her sinks, a large tub with a view, and a separate standing shower combine to create both a retreat and a remedy for hectic mornings.

- **Secondary Bedrooms:** Bedroom 2 has plenty of closet space and would be perfect for a nursery or even a converted office. Bedroom 3 also has ample closet space and is opened up by a vaulted ceiling. Both are in a space of their own with a nearby full bathroom.

CAD FILE AVAILABLE

Clean lines and a layout fit for contemporary living create a graceful and efficient update to a simple cottage design that is perfect for families just starting out.

Features:

- **Great Room:** At the center of everything, this great room will be the heart of the home. Its unhampered transition into the dining areas and kitchen creates a feeling of openness that will welcome guests into your home.

- **Kitchen:** This kitchen maximizes space and efficiency with simple transitions and plenty of workspace. The laundry room is adjacent for easy cleanup; the dining room and breakfast area are just steps away; and a snack bar provides the only barrier between the kitchen and great room. Cookouts are also simplified by easy access to the back patio.

Patio

MBr
14-5x11-6
vaulted clg

Brk fst
9-7x 10-8

Great Rm
13-0x21-5
vaulted clg

Dining

Kit
9-3x 11-0

Br 2
9-0x 9-0

Dn

Garage
18-4x20-4

Br 3
10-8x9-8
vaulted clg

Entry

Porch

46'-0"

38'-0"

Copyright by designer/architect.

Images provided by designer/architect.

Plan #F01-171001

Dimensions: 44' W x 41' D
Levels: 1
Heated Square Footage: 1,277
Bedrooms: 3
Bathrooms: 2
Foundation: Crawl space or slab
Materials List Available: No
Price Category: B

You'll love this design if you're looking for a compact ranch with rustic, country styling and plenty of well designed family areas.

Features:

- **Porch:** Set a couple of rockers and containers of blooming plants and fragrant herbs on this lovely covered front porch.

- **Great Room:** A substantial fireplace is the focal point of this large room. Fill it with a dried floral bouquet in summer, and gather chairs around its warmth in winter.

- **Dining Room:** This room adjoins the great room for easy entertaining in any season and opens to the large covered porch for summer parties.

- **Kitchen:** With good counter space and an open layout, this kitchen is built for efficiency.

- **Master Bedroom:** Split from the other two bedrooms for privacy, this quiet retreat features a large walk-in closet and private bath.

Copyright by designer/architect.

Plan #F01-121012

Dimensions: 40' W x 48'8" D

Levels: 1

Heated Square Footage: 1,195

Bedrooms: 3

Bathrooms: 2

Foundation: Basement;
crawl space or slab for fee

Materials List Available: Yes

Price Category: B

This home, as shown in the photograph, may differ from the actual blueprints. For more detailed information, please check the floor plans carefully.

CAD FILE AVAILABLE

This compact one-level home uses an open plan to make the most of its square footage.

Features:

- Ceiling Height: 8 ft.
- Covered Porch: This delightful area, located off the kitchen, provides a private spot to enjoy some fresh air.
- Open Plan: The family room dining area and kitchen share a big open space to provide a sense of spaciousness. Moving so easily

between these interrelated areas provides the convenience demanded by a busy lifestyle.

- Master Suite: An open plan is convenient, but it is still important for everyone to have their private space. The master suite enjoys its own bath and walk-in closet. The secondary bedrooms share a nearby bath.
- Garage: Here you will find parking for two cars and plenty of extra storage space as well.

Rendering reflects floor plan

Images provided by designer/architect.

Plan #F01-271007

Dimensions: 51'5" W x 40'9" D

Levels: 1

Heated Square Footage: 1,283

Bedrooms: 3

Bathrooms: 2

Foundation: Basement

Materials List Available: Yes

Price Category: B

This charming traditional home has an appealing exterior and is full of exceptional interior features.

Features:

- Great Room: This room is just off of the front foyer and boasts a dramatic vaulted ceiling and inviting fireplace.

- Dining room: Open to the great room, this area overlooks the delightful rear deck.

- Kitchen: This area is efficiently designed with a pantry and a sunny vaulted breakfast nook, which leads to the deck, making breakfast alfresco a daily option.

Images provided by designer/architect.

Plan #F01-401024

Dimensions: 70' W x 36' D

Levels: 1

Heated Square Footage: 1,298

Bedrooms: 3

Bathrooms: 2

Foundation: Basement

Materials List Available: Yes

Price Category: B

A front veranda, cedar lattice, and a solid-stone chimney enhance the appeal of this one-story country-style home.

Features:

- Great Room: The open plan begins with the great room, which includes a fireplace and a plant ledge over the wall separating the living space from the country kitchen.

- Country Kitchen: This U-shaped kitchen provides an island work counter and sliding glass doors to the rear deck and screened porch.

- Master Suite: This area has a wall closet and a private bath with window seat.

Optional Floor Plan

Left Elevation

Right Elevation

Rear Elevation

Images provided by designer/architect.

Plan #F01-391008

Dimensions: 50' W x 40' D

Levels: 1

Heated Square Footage: 1,312

Bedrooms: 3

Bathrooms: 2

Foundation: Crawl space, slab, or basement

Materials List Available: Yes

Price Category: B

Here's the sum of brains and beauty, which will please all types of families, from starters and nearly empty nesters to those going golden.

Features:

- Entry: This restful fresh-air porch and formal foyer bring you graciously toward the great room, with its fireplace and vaulted ceiling.

- Dining Room: This adjacent dining room features sliding doors to the deck and smooth open access to the U-shaped kitchen.

- Laundry Room: The laundry area has its own separate landing from the garage, so it's conveniently out of the way.

- Master Suite: This master suite with a tray ceiling features nearly "limitless" closet space, a private bath, and a large hall linen closet.

- Bedrooms: The two secondary bedrooms, also with roomy closets, share a full bath. Bedroom 3 easily becomes a home office with direct foyer access and a window overlooking the porch.

Crawl Space Option

Plan #F01-161004

Dimensions: 50' W x 54'8" D

Levels: 1

Heated Square Footage: 1,315

Bedrooms: 3

Bathrooms: 2

Foundation: Basement

Materials List Available: Yes

Price Category: B

This multi-featured ranch has a covered porch, a ceiling that slopes to an 11-ft. height, an optional library, and a full basement to enhance your living enjoyment.

Features:

- **Great Room:** Experience the expansive entertainment area created by this open great room and the dining area. Enjoy the lovely fireplace, with full glass on both sides.

- **Kitchen:** This kitchen is designed for total convenience and easy work patterns with immediate access to the first-floor laundry area.

- **Master Bedroom:** This master bedroom, split from the other bedrooms, offers privacy and features tray ceiling design.

- **Basement:** Designed with the future in mind, this full basement has an open staircase leading to it and can be updated to expand your living space.

Images provided by designer/architect.

Deck

Master Bedroom 12'-4" x 13'-0"

Great Room 18'-8" x 17'-4"

Bedroom 11'-4" x 10'-8"

Bath

Bath

Dining

Laun.

Kitchen 13'-4" x 9'-11"

Foyer

Bedroom 12'-4" x 10'-10"

Porch

Garage 20'-0" x 26'-2"

Copyright by designer/architect.

54'-8"

50'-0"

Bath

Optional Library Floor Plan

Rear Elevation

Left Elevation

Right Elevation

Images provided by designer/architect.

Plan #F01-121121

Dimensions: 47'4" W x 45'8" D
Levels: 1
Heated Square Footage: 1,341
Bedrooms: 3
Bathrooms: 2
Foundation: Basement;
crawl space or slab for fee
Materials List Available: Yes
Price Category: C

This traditional home is charming and bound to make your life simpler with all of its amenities.

Features:

- Great Room: Already equipped with an entertainment center, bookcase and a fireplace by which you can enjoy those books, this room has endless possibilities. This is a room that will bring the whole family together.

- Kitchen: This design includes everything you need and everything you want: a pantry waiting to be filled with your favorite foods, plenty of workspace, and a snack bar that acts s a useful transition between kitchen and breakfast room.

- Breakfast Room: An extension of the kitchen, this room will fill with the aroma of coffee and a simmering breakfast, so you'll be immersed in your relaxing morning. With peaceful daylight streaming in through a window-lined wall, this will easily become the best part of your day.

- Master Suite: Plenty of breathing room for both of you, there will be no fighting for sink or closet space in this bathroom. The full master bath includes a double-bowl vanity, and the walk-in closet will hold everything you both need. Another perk of this bathroom is the whirlpool bathtub.

- Garage: This two-car garage opens directly into the entry of this home, so there is no reason to get out of your warm, dry car and into unpleasant weather.

Copyright by designer/architect.

Plan #F01-181727

Dimensions: 60' W x 30' D

Levels: 1

Heated Square Footage: 1,350

Bedrooms: 3

Bathrooms: 1

Foundation: Basement;
crawl space or slab for fee

Materials List Available: Yes

Price Category: G

*Images provided by
designer/architect.*

**CAD FILE
CAD
AVAILABLE**

*Copyright by
designer/architect.*

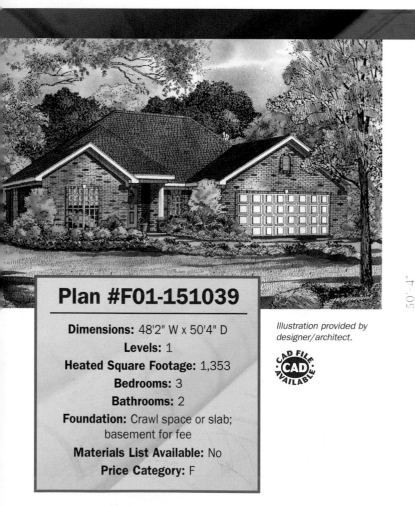

Plan #F01-151039

Dimensions: 48'2" W x 50'4" D

Levels: 1

Heated Square Footage: 1,353

Bedrooms: 3

Bathrooms: 2

Foundation: Crawl space or slab;
basement for fee

Materials List Available: No

Price Category: F

*Illustration provided by
designer/architect.*

**CAD FILE
CAD
AVAILABLE**

*Copyright by
designer/architect.*

Copyright by designer/architect.

Mas. Suite 14x12-6 12 vaulted clg

Br 2 12x10

Patio

Den/ Br 3 11x9

Kit/Brkfst 19x10-8 12 vltd clg

Dining

Garage 21-4x19-4

Great Room 19x18 12 vaulted clg

48'-4"

48'-4"

Plan #F01-271005

Images provided by designer/architect.

Dimensions: 48'4" W x 48'4" D

Levels: 1

Heated Square Footage: 1,368

Bedrooms: 3

Bathrooms: 2

Foundation: Basement

Materials List Available: Yes

Price Category: B

SMARTtip

Design with Computers

Consider using a computer-aided design (CAD) program to plan your deck. Some programs let you see three-dimensional views of your design complete with railings, stairs, planters, hot tubs, and the surrounding landscaping.

Plan #F01-401033

Images provided by designer/architect.

CAD FILE AVAILABLE

Dimensions: 62' W x 29' D

Levels: 1

Heated Square Footage: 1,405

Bedrooms: 3

Bathrooms: 2

Foundation: Crawl space or basement

Materials List Available: Yes

Price Category: B

Copyright by designer/architect.

W.I.C.

k

din 10'6x10'4 VAULTED

10'6x10'4 VAULTED

EATING BAR

EXPOSED BEAM

EXPOSED BEAM

br2 10'x12'8 VAULTED

br3 8'10x9'4 VAULTED

WOODSTOVE

grt rm 21'x17'8 VAULTED

W.I.C.

mbr 12'2x13'8 VAULTED

DECK

Rear Elevation

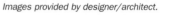

Plan #F01-321013

Dimensions: 68' W x 30' D

Levels: 1

Heated Square Footage: 1,360

Bedrooms: 3

Bathrooms: 2

Foundation: Basement

Materials List Available: Yes

Price Category: B

This efficiently designed home has an abundance of space for the growing family.

Features:

• Covered Porch: This large covered front porch welcomes you home, providing the perfect place to sit and relax.

• Family Room: With its large size, cozy fireplace, and convenient connection to the kitchen, this family room is wonderful for both entertaining and relaxing.

• Kitchen: You will love to cook in this beautiful kitchen, which features a pantry and an island.

• Master Suite: Located in the rear of the home, this spacious master suite features a large bath and a walk-in closet. Window placement allows for many possible furniture arrangements.

• Secondary Bedrooms: Equal-size rooms will help eliminate quarrels on who has the larger room. Both rooms feature large closets.

Images provided by designer/architect.

Plan #F01-251003

Dimensions: 42' W x 42' D

Levels: 1

Heated Square Footage: 1,393

Bedrooms: 3

Bathrooms: 2

Foundation: Crawl space or slab

Materials List Available: Yes

Price Category: B

Come home to this three-bedroom home with front porch and unattached garage.

Features:

- **Family Room:** This room feels large and warm, with its high ceiling and cozy fireplace.

- **Kitchen:** This island kitchen with dining area has plenty of cabinet space as well as a convenient built-in desk.

- **Master Bedroom:** This master bedroom is tucked away in the rear of this home and features a large walk-in closet and a view of the backyard.

- **Master Bath:** Located in the rear of the home, this master bath features a soaking tub and a separate shower.

Plan #F01-131014

Dimensions: 48' W x 43'4" D
Levels: 1
Heated Square Footage: 1,380
Bedrooms: 3
Bathrooms: 2
Foundation: Crawl space or slab; basement or walkout for fee
Materials List Available: No
Price Category: C

Images provided by designer/architect.

The exterior of this home looks formal, thanks to its twin dormers, gables, and the bay windows that flank the columned porch, but the inside is contemporary in both design and features.

Features:

- Great Room: Centrally located, this great room has a 10-ft. ceiling. A fireplace, built-in cabinets, and windows that overlook the rear covered porch make it as practical as it is attractive.

- Dining Room: A bay window adds to the charm of this versatile room.

- Kitchen: This U-shaped room is designed to make cooking and cleaning jobs efficient.

- Master Suite: With a bay window, a walk-in closet, and a private bath with an oval tub, the master suite may be your favorite area.

- Additional Bedrooms: Located on the opposite side of the house from the master suite, these rooms share a full bath in the hall.

Living Room

DECK

9' CLG
DINING RM
11'-0" ×
15'-4"

KITCHEN
9'-0" ×
10'-0"

OPTIONAL TWO CAR GARAGE

20'-0" × 20'-0"

Copyright by
designer/architect.

BEDRM #3
11'-4" ×
10'-0"

COV. PORCH

SL GL DRS

LAUN
RM

W D PANT

BUILT-IN

CL LIN

BATH #2

CL LIN

UP

UTIL

WICL

10' CLG
GREAT RM
20'-0" × 15'-4"

FIREPLACE

OPT. BSMT ENTRY

CL

MSTR BATH

BEDRM #2
11'-4" ×
12'-4"

CL

COV. PORCH

CL

TRAY CEIL
MSTR BEDRM
12'-0" ×
16'-4"

UP

FUTURE EXPANSION
20'-0" × 15'-4"

DN

DN

Bonus Area

Living Room

Rear Elevation

Plan #F01-321002

Dimensions: 72' W x 28' D

Levels: 1

Heated Square Footage: 1,400

Bedrooms: 3

Bathrooms: 2

Foundation: Crawl space, basement

Materials List Available: Yes

Price Category: D

If you're looking for a well-designed compact home with contemporary amenities, this could be the home of your dreams.

Features:

- Covered Porch: Just the right size for some rockers and a swing, this porch could become your outdoor living area when the weather is fine.

- Living Room: A vaulted ceiling adds to the spacious feeling in this room, where friends and family are sure to gather.

- Kitchen: This space-saving design, in combination with the ample counter and cabinet space, makes cooking a pleasure.

- Utility Room: This large room is fitted with cabinets for extra storage space. You'll find storage space in the large garage, too.

- Master Bedroom: This room is somewhat secluded for privacy, making it an ideal place for some quiet time at the end of the day.

Images provided by designer/architect.

CAD FILE AVAILABLE

SMARTtip

Fabric Draping Ability

Test a fabric's draping ability by looking at a large piece in a fabric store. Gather at least two to three yards of material, holding one end in your hand. Check how it drapes. Does it fall into folds easily? Also look at the pattern when it is gathered. Does the design become lost in the folds? Ask a salesclerk or a friend to hold the fabric, and look at it from a few feet away.

Images provided by designer/architect.

Plan #F01-351009

Dimensions: 54' W x 47' D

Levels: 1

Heated Square Footage: 1,400

Bedrooms: 3

Bathrooms: 2

Foundation: Crawl space, slab, or basement

Materials List Available: No

Price Category: F

This design offers a great value in space planning by using the open concept, with split bedrooms, in a layout that is easy to build.

Features:

• Ceilings: All ceilings are a minimum of 9-ft. high.

• Great Room: This large gathering area provides room for family activities as well as being open to the kitchen and dining area.

• Master Suite: This oversized private area provides a great bathroom arrangement for busy couples as well as a large walk-in closet.

• Bedrooms: The split bedroom layout provides zoned privacy and improved noise control.

• Patio: This area is the perfect place to enjoy the afternoons grilling out or relaxing with friends and family.

Copyright by designer/architect.

Under 1,500 sq. ft.

Images provided by designer/architect.

CAD FILE AVAILABLE

Plan #F01-401025

Dimensions: 70' W x 34' D

Levels: 1

Heated Square Footage: 1,408

Bedrooms: 3

Bathrooms: 2

Foundation: Crawl space or basement

Materials List Available: Yes

Price Category: B

Optional Floor Plan

Copyright by designer/architect.

DECK

SOAKER TUB   BOX WINDOW

WORKSHOP

country k
18'11 x 13'4
vaulted

WORK ISLAND

mbr
12' x 14'4

SKYLIGHT

two-car garage
21'6 x 19'6

POT LEDGE OVER CLOSETS

grt rm
20' x 13'4
vaulted

ART NICHE

br3
12' x 10'

br2
12' x 10'

VERANDAH

RAILING

Rear Elevation

Plan #F01-341128

Images provided by designer/architect.

CAD FILE AVAILABLE

Dimensions: 76'10" W x 40'10" D

Levels: 1

Heated Square Footage: 1,410

Bedrooms: 3

Bathrooms: 2

Foundation: Crawl space; basement or slab for fee

Materials List Available: Yes

Price Category: B

DECK
12'-0" X 10'-0"

UP TO ATTIC

UTILITIES

GARAGE
23'-2" X 25'-2"

KITCHEN/DINING
21'-11" X 11'-2"

BEDROOM 3
10'-0" X 11'-2"

BEDROOM 2
10'-1" X 11'-2"

BATH 2

Copyright by designer/architect.

DECORATIVE COLUMN

PREFAB FIREPLACE

FAMILY ROOM
16'-7" X 13'-0"

BATH 1

PORCH

BEDROOM 1
15'-2" X 13'-2"

VAULTED CEILING

40'-10"

76'-10"

Images provided by designer/architect.

Copyright by designer/architect.

DINE · **D. W.** · **KIT. 9'-6"x8'-8"** · **MUD RM.** · **S.** · **HTR. CLO. PLAN - 2 STORAGE** · **FAMILY AREA 25'-6"x12'** · **BEDROOM 11'x9'-4"** · **BEDROOM 11'-2"-10'-4"** · **dn.** · **P** · **GARAGE 19'-10"x 20'** · **LIVING ROOM 21'x13'** · **MASTER BEDROOM 11'-2"x13'-7"** · **BATH** · **STOR.** · **PORCH** · **BATH** · 66'-0" · 30'-0"

Plan #F01-321330

Dimensions: 66' W x 30' D

Levels: 1

Heated Square Footage: 1,414

Bedrooms: 3

Bathrooms: 2

Foundation: Crawl space, slab or basement

Materials List Available: Yes

Price Category: B

CAD FILE AVAILABLE

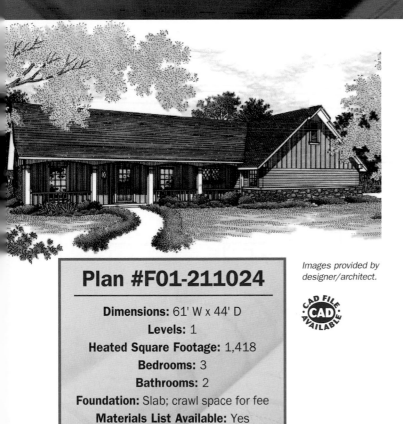

Images provided by designer/architect.

Copyright by designer/architect.

patio · **br 3 12 x 11** · **living 18 x 18** · **mbr 16 x 14** · **lin** · **bath** · **clo** · **bath** · **lin** · **br 2 12 x 12** · **foy** · **dining 12 x 11** · **kit 12x9** · **ref** · **w d** · **sto** · **garage 22 x 22** · **porch 39 x 6**

Plan #F01-211024

Dimensions: 61' W x 44' D

Levels: 1

Heated Square Footage: 1,418

Bedrooms: 3

Bathrooms: 2

Foundation: Slab; crawl space for fee

Materials List Available: Yes

Price Category: B

CAD FILE AVAILABLE

Plan #F01-341064

Dimensions: 58'6" W x 36'9" D

Levels: 1

Heated Square Footage: 1,418

Bedrooms: 3

Bathrooms: 2

Foundation: Crawl space; slab
or basement for fee

Materials List Available: Yes

Price Category: C

*Images provided by
designer/architect.*

CAD FILE AVAILABLE

*Copyright by
designer/architect.*

Plan #F01-121009

Dimensions: 50' W x 58' D

Levels: 1

Heated Square Footage: 1,422

Bedrooms: 3

Bathrooms: 2

Foundation: Basement;
crawl space or slab for fee

Materials List Available: Yes

Price Category: B

*Images provided by
designer/architect.*

CAD FILE AVAILABLE

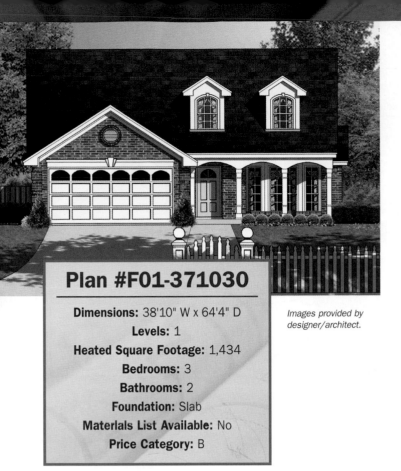

Plan #F01-371030

Dimensions: 38'10" W x 64'4" D

Levels: 1

Heated Square Footage: 1,434

Bedrooms: 3

Bathrooms: 2

Foundation: Slab

Materlals List Available: No

Price Category: B

Images provided by designer/architect.

Copyright by designer/architect.

Plan #F01-371049

Dimensions: 52' W x 45' D

Levels: 1

Heated Square Footage: 1,440

Bedrooms: 3

Bathrooms: 2

Foundation: Slab or crawl space

Materials List Available: No

Price Category: B

Images provided by designer/architect.

Copyright by designer/architect.

Images provided by designer/architect.

Plan #F01-221016

Dimensions: 56' W x 42' D

Levels: 1

Heated Square Footage: 1,461

Bedrooms: 3

Bathrooms: 2

Foundation: Basement

Materials List Available: No

Price Category: B

The interesting roofline and classic siding give this traditional ranch home an instant appeal.

Features:

- Ceiling Height: 8 ft.

- Great Room: From the entry, you'll look into this great room, where a handsome fireplace with large flanking windows makes you feel at home.

- Dining Room: Open to the great room, this room features access to the rear deck. An eating island shared with the kitchen allows the whole living area to flow together.

- Kitchen: The step-saving layout and ample counter space will delight the family chef.

- Master Suite: With a large walk-in closet and deluxe bath with a whirlpool tub, separate shower, and a two-sink vanity, this area will become a real retreat at the end of the day.

- Additional Bedrooms: Add the optional door from the entry to transform bedroom #2 into a quiet den, or use it as a bedroom.

WOOD DECK
20'0" × 10'0"

MBR.
12'10" × 15'0"

GRT. RM.
CATHEDRAL CEILING
14'6" × 19'0"

DIN.
CATH. CLG.
10'6" × 11'4"

KIT.
CATH. CLG.
11'0" × 11'4"

BR. #2/
DEN
11'0" × 11'0"

2 CAR GARAGE
19'8" × 23'4"

BR. #3
10'0" × 10'6"

Copyright by designer/architect.

42'-0"

56'-0"

Rear Elevation

Plan #F01-131003

Dimensions: 60' W x 39'10" D
Levels: 1
Heated Square Footage: 1,466
Bedrooms: 3
Bathrooms: 2
Foundation: Crawl space or slab;
basement for fee
Materials List Available: No
Price Category: C

Images provided by designer/architect.

Victorian styling adds elegance to this compact and easy-to-maintain ranch design.

Features:

- Ceiling Height: 8 ft.

- Foyer: Bridging between the front door and the great room, this foyer is a surprise feature.

- Great Room: A 10-ft. stepped ceiling adds to the spacious feeling of this room, while the corner fireplace gives it an intimate feeling. Large sliding glass doors at the rear of the room open to the backyard.

- Dining Room: This formal room adjoins the great room, allowing guests and family to flow between the rooms.

- Breakfast Room: Turrets add a Victorian feeling to this room that's just off of the kitchen and overlooks the front porch.

- Master Suite: Privacy is assured in this suite, which is separated from the main part of the house. A compartmented bath and large walk-in closet add convenience to its beauty.

Breakfast Room

Images provided by designer/architect.

Plan #F01-151529

Dimensions: 43' W x 66'6" D

Levels: 1

Heated Square Footage: 1,474

Bedrooms: 2

Bathrooms: 2

Foundation: Crawl space or slab; basement or walkout for fee

Materials List Available: No

Price Category: F

This elegant design is reflective of the Arts and Crafts era. Copper roofing and carriage style garage doors warmly welcome guests into this split-bedroom plan.

Features:

- **Great Room:** With access to the grilling porch as a bonus, this large gathering area features a 10-ft.-high ceiling and a beautiful fireplace.

- **Kitchen:** This fully equipped island kitchen has a raised bar and a built-in pantry. The area is open to the great room and dining room, giving an open and airy feeling to the home.

- **Master Suite:** Located on the opposite side of the home from the secondary bedroom, this retreat offers a large sleeping area and two large closets. The master bath features a spa tub, a separate shower, and dual vanities.

- **Bedroom:** This secondary bedroom has a large closet and access to the full bathroom in the hallway.

Front View

Plan #F01-131017

Dimensions: 69'8" W x 39'4" D
Levels: 1
Heated Square Footage: 1,480
Bedrooms: 3
Bathrooms: 2
Foundation: Crawl space or slab; basement for fee
Materials List Available: Yes
Price Category: C

This fully accessible home is designed for wheelchair access to every area, giving everyone true enjoyment and freedom of movement.

Features:

- **Great Room:** Facing towards the rear, this great room features a volume ceiling that adds to the spacious feeling of the room.

- **Kitchen:** Designed for total convenience and easy work patterns, this kitchen also offers a view out to the covered front porch.

- **Master Bedroom:** Enjoy the quiet in this room which is sure to become your favorite place to relax at the end of the day.

- **Additional Bedrooms:** Both rooms have easy access to a full bath and feature nicely sized closet spaces.

- **Garage:** Use the extra space in this attached garage for storage.

Images provided by designer/architect.

Plan Layout with Optional Basement

Alternate Bath
Non Accessible

Rear Elevation

Images provided by designer/architect.

Plan #F01-341023

Dimensions: 72'7" W x 34' D

Levels: 1

Heated Square Footage: 1,469

Bedrooms: 3

Bathrooms: 2

Foundation: Crawl space; basement or slab for fee

Materials List Available: Yes

Price Category: C

Plan #F01-181153

Dimensions: 46' W x 34' D

Levels: 1

Heated Square Footage: 1,478

Bedrooms: 3

Bathrooms: 1

Foundation: Basement; crawl space or slab for fee

Materials List Available: Yes

Price Category: E

Images provided by designer/architect.

Plan #F01-281031

Dimensions: 48' W x 58' D

Levels: 1

Heated Square Footage: 1,493

Bedrooms: 3

Bathrooms: 2

Foundation: Walkout; crawl space, slab or basement for fee

Materials List Available: Yes

Price Category: B

Images provided by designer/architect.

Rear Elevation

Plan #F01-221013

Dimensions: 48' W x 58'8" D

Levels: 1

Heated Square Footage: 1,495

Bedrooms: 3

Bathrooms: 2

Foundation: Basement

Materials List Available: No

Price Category: B

Illustration provided by designer/architect.

Rear Elevation

Plan #F01-351020

Dimensions: 54' W x 48' D

Levels: 1

Heated Square Footage: 1,488

Bedrooms: 3

Bathrooms: 3

Foundation: Basement

Materials List Available: Yes

Price Category: F

CAD FILE AVAILABLE

Images provided by designer/architect.

This is a lot of house for its size and is an excellent example of the popular split bedroom layout.

Features:

• Great Room: This large room is open to the dining room and features a large coat closet.

• Kitchen: This fully equipped kitchen has a peninsula counter, rear view to the patio and is open into the dining room.

• Master Suite: This private area, located on the other side of the home from the secondary bedrooms, features large walk-in closets, and bath areas, one with a garden tub and the other with a shower.

• Bedrooms: The two secondary bedrooms have large closets and share a hall bathroom.

Plan #F01-761048

Dimensions: 44' W x 53' 4"D
Levels: 1
Heated Square Footage: 1,615
Bedrooms: 2
Bathrooms: 2
Foundation: Basement
Materials List Available: Yes
Price Category: B

With its refreshing, open floor plan and Craftsman-inspired exterior, this home is a popular style.

Features:

- Great Room: The sizable great room enjoys a fireplace surrounded in shelves as well as a wall of windows for taking in views of the outdoors.

- Breakfast/Dining Area: The breakfast/dining area is just steps from the functional kitchen with a corner walk-in pantry, and a wrap-around counter with dining space for up to five people.

- Master Bedroom: The master bedroom has a cheerful atmosphere thanks to five windows and it includes an oversized private bath with a corner whirlpool tub.

Patio

Brkfst/ Dining
12-8x14-11

Great Rm
16-9x21-11
12' Clg

MBr
12-8x14-6
Coffer Clg

Kitchen
12-8x12-9

Dn

Garage
22-8x24-0

Foyer

Br 2
12-8x11-0

Porch

Copyright by designer/architect.

Plan #F01-401022

Dimensions: 59' W x 33' D

Levels: 1

Heated Square Footage: 1,495

Bedrooms: 3

Bathrooms: 2

Foundation: Crawl space

Materials List Available: Yes

Price Category: B

This three-bedroom cottage has just the right rustic mix of vertical wood siding and stone accents. Inside, the living is pure resort-style comfort.

Features:

- High Ceilings: Vaulted ceilings are featured throughout the living room and master bedroom of this unique home.

- Living Room: This room has a fireplace and full-height windows overlooking the deck.

- Dining Room: This room features double-door access to the deck

- Master Bedroom: This principal sleeping area has a single door that opens to the deck.

- Bedrooms: Two family bedrooms share a bathroom that is situated between them.

Images provided by designer/architect.

CAD FILE AVAILABLE

Copyright by designer/architect.

stor

br2 10'2 x 10'

br3 9' x 10'

kit 10' x 11'4

din 9' x 11'4

VAULTED CLG.

mbr 13' x 14'8

VAULTED CLG.

liv 25' x 15'6

DECK

Rear Elevation

Right Elevation

Left Elevation

Images provided by designer/architect.

Plan #F01-161079

Dimensions: 66'4" W x 44'10" D

Levels: 1

Heated Square Footage: 1,498

Bedrooms: 3

Bathrooms: 2

Foundation: Basement; crawl space or slab for fee

Materials List Available: Yes

Price Category: B

This three-bedroom one-story house enjoys step-saving convenience, plus a beautiful stone and siding facade with a covered porch.

Features:

- **Great Room:** This gathering area, with a gas fireplace and sloped ceiling, is visible from the foyer, breakfast room, and kitchen, creating a large open area.

- **Kitchen:** This large kitchen, with its snack bar, and the breakfast area both open generously to the great room for a continuous traffic flow.

- **Master Suite:** This suite enjoys a luxurious bath, large walk-in closet, and raised ceiling.

- **Basement:** This full basement shows a rough-in for a bathroom and offers space for a future living area allowing plenty of space to grow.

Rear Elevation

Retaining Walls

Retaining walls let you alter the grade or slope of the land to create level areas that you can use for planting, adding a patio, or any one of a number of uses. They also protect the slope from eroding or collapsing. As with freestanding stone walls, you can build a dry-laid wall or a mortared version. Dry-laid walls are informal and do not require a concrete footing, so they are easier to build than mortared retaining walls. Mortared walls offer more stability, but they tend to be more difficult to build.

The walls in the sunken garden, shown below, are a good example of retaining wall construction. With thoughtful, creative planning you can build a dry-laid retaining wall that is handsome, durable, and an asset to your landscape.

A loose-laid wall, opposite, provides an informal touch by softening the perimeter of this garden.

Retaining walls create a sunken garden room, below, that extends the normal growing season.

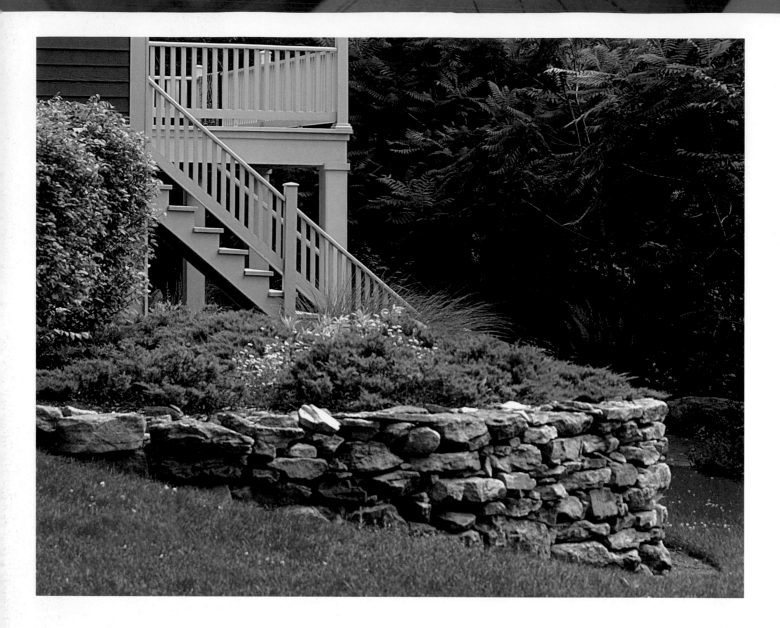

Preparing the Site

Begin by calculating the height of the wall. Usually, the angle of the slope determines the height of the wall — the steeper the slope the taller the wall. There are exceptions to this rule. For example, privacy walls are usually tall no matter how steep the slope against which they are built. You may want a wall at a specific height so that you can get access to a garden bed.

Tall walls are more difficult and more costly to build. Structural and drainage issues are more critical for walls more than 3 feet tall and, if you have no prior experience, should not be attempted without professional advice or assistance. The visual mass of a tall wall can also present problems. Rather than build one tall wall, consider adding terraces and building a series of shorter walls.

Walls and Permits
Before you start digging, find out whether you need a permit to build a dry-laid stone retaining wall.

Terracing a Slope. Farmers have been terracing hillsides for thousands of years. For a homeowner, the incentive usually comes from a desire to turn an otherwise uninspiring or difficult-to-maintain hillside into accessible and attractive gardens.

The shorter walls typical of terraces require less skill to fabricate, and you can construct them in stages. Terraces are also less expensive to construct than one tall wall, and they create an inviting destination. All the steps that apply to retaining walls apply to terracing a natural hillside or constructed berm. If the slope is steep and you want wide terraces, then you will have extra fill to remove from the site.

Excavation. Once you know the location and height of the wall, you are ready to begin excavating the site. Short walls with little slope behind them may require nothing more than removing the sod and excavating down 4 to 6 inches. On sloped ground, excavation is usually a cut-and-fill process. As you cut into the slope, you use the soil to level off another area.

Plan on excavating more soil than may appear necessary. You will need space for the wall, space to work, room for gravel backfill, and space for additional backfill to minimize pressure on the wall — an important consideration for walls that front steep, tall slopes.

In many cases, you will end up with more soil than you can use on the current project. Try to find some other landscaping use for the removed soil.

The Base of the Wall. Because they can shift with the movement of the earth, dry-laid retaining walls do not require a concrete footing. In gravelly soil that drains well,

remove the sod and 4 to 6 inches of topsoil. Slope the grade in the trench ¼ to ½ inch per foot into the hill. In sandy or wet soils, excavate an additional 4 to 12 inches; lay down landscape fabric; and backfill the trench with gravel that compacts and drains.

The height of the wall will determine the width of your trench. Use this guide: for walls under 3 feet tall, make the width of the wall at its base equal to one-half the finished height of the wall; for taller walls, the width of the base should be closer to two-thirds the height of the wall. A 3-foot-tall wall should have a 2-foot-wide base. Consult a professional mason or landscape contractor when planning on a wall that is taller than 3 feet.

Mortared walls require a concrete footing. Local building codes determine the depth and width of the footing.

Drainage. Runoff from the slope will seep out between the stones of a dry-laid retaining wall. Typically, these types of walls do not require an additional drainage system. But if the

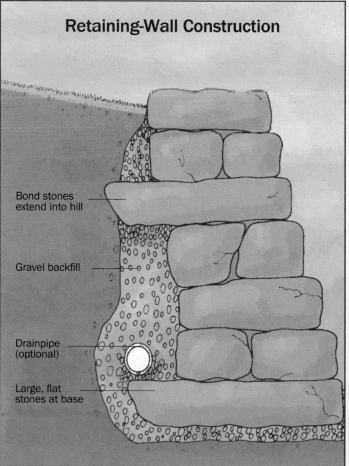

Use retaining walls to create level areas for planting, as shown opposite. The height of some parts of the wall makes it easy to tend to the plants.

Building with large, rounded stones is challenging and best used on short walls, left.

Retaining-Wall Construction

Bond stones extend into hill

Gravel backfill

Drainpipe (optional)

Large, flat stones at base

site is wet and you want to minimize seepage through the wall, add a drainpipe that can move the water away from the wall. Backfilling with a few inches of coarse gravel minimizes erosion and loss of soil through the wall. For greater stability, particularly with steep slopes, lay landscape fabric between the soil and the backfill gravel.

If you are planning a mortared wall, you must provide a drainage system. Without weep holes or some other drainage system, runoff from the slope will exert tremendous pressure against the wall, resulting in buckling of the wall.

Building the Wall

When the stone is delivered to the site, sort it as you would for a freestanding wall: larger stones for the base, bond stones to span between wythes, rubble for fill between the wythes, and cap stones or coping for the top of the wall. Unlike freestanding walls, retaining walls need only one good face. If your wall is short and there isn't a lot of pressure on it, you can build the wall one stone wide provided your stones are large and good building stone, that is, they fit together well.

Calculate the Batter. Retaining walls lean back into the slope they support. This lean is called the batter. Retaining walls typically have about a 2-inch batter for every foot of height. If a wall is short and the stone is at least semidressed, you can reduce or eliminate the batter.

Lay the Base Course. Use your largest and flattest stones for the base course. Place bond stones at each end of the wall and at 4- to 6-foot intervals along the wall. Ideally, the bond stones should be long enough to extend into the slope. Between the bond stones, lay wall stones, one in front of the other, to create a double-wythe wall. Fill any gaps between these stones with smaller stones or rubble.

Tilt all the main wall stones into the hill. After laying the first course, you can backfill along the front of the wall and firmly tamp the soil in 2-inch layers. If you are going to install perforated drainpipe, now is the time to lay it along the backside of the wall. Slope the pipe to facilitate drainage.

Add the Remaining Courses. Place the next course, setting it back slightly from the first. Stagger the location of the bond stones, offsetting them from the bond stones in the first course. Lay stones so that all joints between courses are staggered.

After the second course is laid, backfill with gravel and fill almost to the top of the second course. Firmly tamp the gravel in 2-inch layers. Continue laying up courses in the same manner, checking the angle of the face with your batter gauge periodically and backfilling after every two courses.

Cap the Wall. Cap stones usually span the width of the wall and protrude slightly over it. Because water can move through a dry-laid wall, the water-shedding function of the cap stones isn't as crucial. For stability, especially if the wall is located

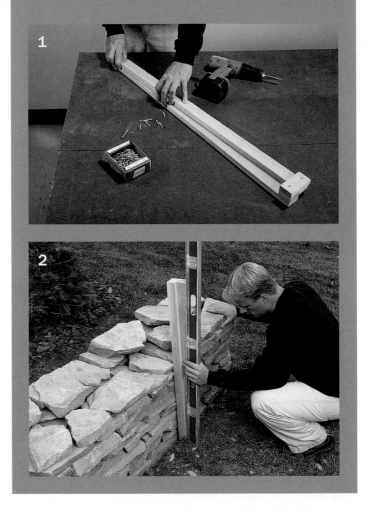

somewhere where it will be used as seating, you may want to mortar the capstones.

Finish Backfilling and Grading. After laying the capstones, backfill with gravel up to within 4 inches or so of the top of the wall. Lay landscape fabric over the top of the gravel, and finish backfilling with soil or mulch.

Retaining walls lean back into the slope. Plan on a 2-in. batter for every foot of height.

This charming water feature, left, is enclosed by an informal-looking stone retaining wall.

Instead of a single high wall, consider building a series of stepped layers, bottom left, that you can then plant.

To facilitate drainage for walls such as the one shown bottom right, as you set the stones, backfill with gravel behind the wall.

order direct: 1-800-523-6789

Lay retaining wall stones so that all joints between courses are staggered, above.

Runoff from the slope will seep out between the stones of a dry-laid retaining wall, right.

Images provided by designer/architect.

Plan #F01-151215

Dimensions: 53' W x 56'6" D
Levels: 1
Heated Square Footage: 1,519
Bedrooms: 3
Bathrooms: 2
Foundation: Crawl space or slab; basement or walkout for fee
Materials List Available: No
Price Category: H

CAD FILE AVAILABLE

This brick home, with a front-loading garage, is the perfect home for a young family.

Features:

• Great Room: This large entertainment area has a corner fireplace, plenty of windows and an entry to the grilling porch.

• Kitchen: Designed with a walk-through layout, this kitchen is open to the breakfast room.

• Master Suite: This private area, located on the opposite side of the home from the secondary bedrooms, features a master bathroom with large double walk-in closets.

• Bedrooms: The two secondary bedrooms share a common bathroom.

Images provided by designer/architect.

Plan #F01-281022

Dimensions: 48' W x 58' D

Levels: 1

Heated Square Footage: 1,506

Bedrooms: 3

Bathrooms: 2

Foundation: Basement;
crawl space for fee

Materials List Available: Yes

Price Category: C

Rear Elevation

You'll spend hours enjoying the sunshine on this home's wraparound porch and gazebo.

Features:

- **Porch:** Stretching from the front to the back of the house, this covered porch has a gazebo on one corner and wraps around to become a covered deck at the back.

- **Great Room:** This beautiful great room is surrounded in windows and includes a three-sided fireplace and French doors that open out onto the porch by the gazebo.

- **Kitchen:** Divided from the dining room and great room by an island with a raised snack bar, this kitchen also has French doors nearby that open out to the covered deck, a wonderful location for outdoor meals.

- **Master Suite:** Close to the secondary bedrooms, this master suite includes a spacious walk-in closet, a whirlpool tub, angled shower and a dual-sink vanity.

Plan #F01-351062

Dimensions: 51'8" W x 51'2" D

Levels: 1

Heated Square Footage: 1,502

Bedrooms: 3

Bathrooms: 2

Foundation: Crawl space or slab

Materials List Available: Yes

Price Category: H

Images provided by designer/architect.

Copyright by designer/architect.

Plan #F01-351005

Dimensions: 61' W x 47'4" D

Levels: 1

Square Footage: 1,501

Bedrooms: 3

Bathrooms: 2

Foundation: Crawl space, slab, or basement

Materials List Available: No

Price Category: H

Images provided by designer/architect.

Images provided by designer/architect.

Copyright by designer/architect.

Plan #F01-501549

Dimensions: 54' W x 60' D

Levels: 1

Heated Square Footage: 1,502

Bedrooms: 3

Bathrooms: 2

Foundation: Crawl space

Materials List Available: Yes

Price Category: C

Images provided by designer/architect.

Copyright by designer/architect.

Rear Elevation

Plan #F01-161003

Dimensions: 60' W x 47' D

Levels: 1

Heated Square Footage: 1,508

Bedrooms: 3

Bathrooms: 2

Foundation: Basement;
crawl space for fee

Materials List Available: Yes

Price Category: C

Plan #F01-161013

Dimensions: 59'4" W x 46'4" D
Levels: 1
Heated Square Footage: 1,509
Bedrooms: 3
Bathrooms: 2
Foundation: Basement
Materials List Available: No
Price Category: C

The unique roofline and stone accents make this home stand apart from the rest.

Features:

- Foyer: Just off the front porch, this entry opens to the great room.

- Great Room: This room warms up with a fireplace and is open to the dining area.

- Kitchen: This kitchen features a peninsula with a raised bar, creating more seating space for the adjacent dining room.

- Master Suite: This suite features a private bathroom with a walk-in closet and a double-bowl vanity.

- Bedrooms: Two secondary bedrooms have large closets and share a hall bathroom.

Images provided by designer/architect.

Right Elevation

Rear Elevation

Left Elevation

Copyright by designer/architect.

Plan #F01-151169

Dimensions: 51'6" W x 49'10" D
Levels: 1
Heated Square Footage: 1,525
Bedrooms: 3
Bathrooms: 2
Foundation: Crawl space or slab; basement or walkout for fee
Materials List Available: No
Price Category: I

This comfortable home is filled with amenities that will thrill both friends and family.

Features:

- **Great Room:** This spacious room has a gas fireplace in the corner, 9-ft. boxed ceiling, and a convenient door to the rear covered porch.

- **Dining Room:** A bay window looks out to the rear porch and lets light flood into this room.

- **Kitchen:** An angled work and snack bar and large pantry are highlights in this well-planned room.

- **Breakfast Room:** A door to the rear porch, wide windows, and a computer desk are highlights here.

- **Master Suite:** You'll feel pampered by the 9-ft. boxed ceiling and bath with two huge closets, whirlpool tub, separate shower, and dual vanity.

- **Additional Bedrooms:** Transform bedroom 3 into a study or home office if you can, and add the optional door to the foyer for total convenience.

Images provided by designer/architect.

Rear View

Images provided by designer/architect.

Plan #F01-401008

Dimensions: 87' W x 44' D

Levels: 1

Heated Square Footage: 1,541

Bedrooms: 3

Bathrooms: 2

Foundation: Basement

Materials List Available: Yes

Price Category: C

This popular design begins with a wraparound covered porch made even more charming by turned wood spindles.

Features:

- Great Room: The entry opens directly into this great room, which is warmed by a woodstove.

- Dining Room: This room offers access to a screened porch for outdoor after-dinner leisure.

- Kitchen: This country kitchen features a center island and a breakfast bay for casual meals.

- Bedrooms: Family bedrooms share a full bath that includes a soaking tub.

Rear Elevation

Left Elevation

Right Elevation

Plan #F01-161010

Dimensions: 50'8" W x 54'2" D
Levels: 1
Heated Square Footage: 1,544
Bedrooms: 3
Bathrooms: 2
Foundation: Basement; slab for fee
Materials List Available: Yes
Price Category: C

Images provided by designer/architect.

This one-story home's many distinctive and elegant features - including arched openings and sloped ceilings - will surprise and excite you at every turn.

Features:

- **Great Room:** Decorative columns frame the entrance from the foyer to the great room and are repeated at the opening to the formal dining area.

- **Kitchen:** Designed for quick meals, or to accommodate an oversized crowd, this kitchen features a curved countertop with seating that functions as a delightful bar.

- **Master Bedroom:** This master bedroom is split to afford you more privacy and features a compartmented bath that forms a separate vanity area.

- **Additional Bedrooms:** Take advantage of the double doors off the foyer to allow one bedroom to function as a library.

Right Elevation

Rear Elevation

Left Elevation

Covered Porch
16' x 10'

WALK-IN CLOSET

Master Bedroom
12' x 14'

Dining
14'2" x 11'8"

ARCHED OPENING

Bath

Great Room
16'4" x 18'

Kitchen
14'2" x 8'10"

Laun.

CURVED CEILING

Hall

Bath

Two-Car Garage
20' x 20'

Foyer

Library/ Bedroom
10'9" x 11'

Bedroom
10' x 11'6"

Copyright by designer/architect.

Porch

50'8"

54'2"

Images provided by designer/architect.

Copyright by designer/architect.

Rear View

Plan #F01-351146

Dimensions: 61' W x 47'4" D

Levels: 1

Heated Square Footage: 1,509

Bedrooms: 3

Bathrooms: 2

Foundation: Crawl space, slab or basement

Materials List Available: Yes

Price Category: H

Images provided by designer/architect.

Plan #F01-321224

Dimensions: 47' W x 45' D

Levels: 1

Heated Square Footage: 1,519

Bedrooms: 4

Bathrooms: 2

Foundation: Crawl space, slab or basement

Materials List Available: Yes

Price Category: C

Plan #F01-151037

Dimensions: 50' W x 56' D

Levels: 1

Heated Square Footage: 1,538

Bedrooms: 3

Bathrooms: 2

Foundation: Crawl space or slab; basement for fee

Materials List Available: No

Price Category: H

CAD FILE AVAILABLE

Plan #F01-391039

Dimensions: 50' W x 45'4" D

Levels: 1

Heated Square Footage: 1,539

Bedrooms: 3

Bathrooms: 2

Foundation: Crawl space, basement or slab

Materials List Available: Yes

Price Category: C

Plan #F01-251004

CAD FILE AVAILABLE

Images provided by designer/architect.

Dimensions: 50'9" W x 42'1" D

Levels: 1

Heated Square Footage: 1,550

Bedrooms: 3

Bathrooms: 2

Foundation: Crawl space or slab

Materials List Available: Yes

Price Category: C

Copyright by designer/architect.

Garage 22 x 22 — 8' Clg.

Storage 16 x 4

Master 16 x 13/7 — Recessed Clg. — 9' Clg.

Rear Porch 24 x 6

Kitchen 12 x 13

Dining 11/8 x 13 — 8' Clg.

Snack Bar

Sloped Ceiling

Br.#3 11 x 10/5 — 8' Clg.

Br.#2 10 x 12 — 8' Clg.

Family Room 21/8 x 15/7 — 12' Clg.

W D

Front Porch 49 x 6 — 8' Clg.

Plan #F01-291001

Images provided by designer/architect.

Dimensions: 63' W x 37' D

Levels: 1

Heated Square Footage: 1,550

Bedrooms: 3

Bathrooms: 2

Foundation: Basement

Materials List Available: No

Price Category: C

DECK

DECK

FP

BEDROOM 11'-0" x 10'-0"

LIVING ROOM 16'-0" x 14'-0"

KITCHEN 12'-0" x 14'-0"

MASTER BEDROOM 16'-0" x 14'-0" — VAULTED CEILING

WIC

BATH

VAULTED CEILING

BATH

BEDROOM 11'-0" x 10'-0"

ENTRY FOYER

DINING ROOM 12'-0" x 14'-0"

DN

FAMILY ENTRY

LAUNDRY

W D

TWO-CAR GARAGE 21'-0" x 21'-0"

PORCH

37'-0"

63'-0"

Copyright by designer/architect.

Rear View

Images provided by designer/architect.

Plan #F01-391021

Dimensions: 54' W x 48'4" D

Levels: 1

Heated Square Footage: 1,568

Bedrooms: 3

Bathrooms: 2

Foundation: Crawl space, basement or slab

Materials List Available: Yes

Price Category: C

Images provided by designer/architect.

Plan #F01-151463

Dimensions: 48'6" W x 56'8" D

Levels: 1

Heated Square Footage: 1,574

Bedrooms: 3

Bathrooms: 2

Foundation: Crawl space or slab; basement or walkout for fee

Materials List Available: No

Price Category: H

Living Room

Images provided by designer/architect.

Copyright by designer/architect.

Plan #F01-191037

Dimensions: 57'4" W x 65' D
Levels: 1
Heated Square Footage: 1,575
Bedrooms: 3
Bathrooms: 2
Foundation: Crawl space or slab
Materials List Available: No
Price Category: E

Images provided by designer/architect.

CAD FILE AVAILABLE

Copyright by designer/architect.

Plan #F01-151608

Dimensions: 49'6" W x 55' D
Levels: 1
Heated Square Footage: 1,576
Bedrooms: 3
Bathrooms: 2
Foundation: Crawl space or slab
Materials List Available: No
Price Category: H

Plan #F01-131007

Dimensions: 59'10" W x 47'8" D
Levels: 1
Heated Square Footage: 1,595
Bedrooms: 3
Bathrooms: 2
Foundation: Crawl space or slab; basement or walkout for fee
Materials List Available: Yes
Price Category: D

Images provided by designer/architect.

Copyright by designer/architect.

Rear Elevation

SMARTtip

Brackets in Window Treatments

Although it is rarely noticed, a bracket plays an important role in supporting rods and poles. If a treatment rubs against a window frame, an extension bracket solves the problem. It projects from the wall at an adjustable length, providing enough clearance. A hold-down bracket anchors a cellular shade or a blind to the bottom of a door, preventing the treatment from moving when the door is opened or closed.

Plan #F01-211030

Dimensions: 75' W x 37' D
Levels: 1
Heated Square Footage: 1,600
Bedrooms: 3
Bathrooms: 2
Foundation: Slab; crawl space or basement for fee
Materials List Available: Yes
Price Category: C

Images provided by designer/architect.

CAD FILE AVAILABLE

Copyright by designer/architect.

Plan #F01-441003

Dimensions: 50' W x 48' D

Levels: 1

Heated Square Footage: 1,580

Bedrooms: 3

Bathrooms: 2½

Foundation: Crawl space; slab or basement available for fee

Materials List Available: No

Price Category: E

Images provided by designer/architect.

Craftsman styling with modern floor planning - that's the advantage of this cozy design. Covered porches at front and back enhance both the look and the livability of the plan.

Features:

- **Great Room:** This vaulted entertaining area boasts a corner fireplace and a built-in media center. The area is open to the kitchen and the dining area.

- **Kitchen:** This large, open island kitchen will please the chef in the family. The raised bar is open to the dining area and the great room.

- **Master Suite:** Look for luxurious amenities such as double sinks and a separate tub and shower in the master bath. The master bedroom has a vaulted ceiling and a walk-in closet with built-in shelves.

- **Bedrooms:** Two secondary bedrooms are located away from the master suite. Each has a large closet and access to a bathroom.

Rear Elevation

Plan #F01-131005

Dimensions: 70' W x 37'4" D
Levels: 1
Heated Square Footage: 1,595
Bedrooms: 3
Bathrooms: 2
Foundation: Crawl space or slab;
basement for fee
Materials List Available: Yes
Price Category: D

Images provided by designer/architect.

With the finest features of an open design in the main living areas, this home gives privacy where you need it. Best of all, it's wheelchair accessible.

Features:

- Foyer: A high ceiling gives this area real presence and serves to blend it seamlessly with the great room and the dining room.

- Great Room: The open design allows you to use this room as an extension of the dining room or, if you wish, furnish it to create a private reading nook or visually separate media center.

- Breakfast Room: Both this room and the adjacent well-appointed kitchen flow into the rest of the living area. However, access to the rear porch, where you can sit out and enjoy the weather while you eat, distinguishes this room.

- Master Suite: Located in the same wing as the other bedrooms, this suite has a separate entrance and features a vaulted ceiling, three closets, and a compartmented bath.

SMARTtip

Create a Courtyard

Create a private walled-garden retreat with fences covered by climbing vines. Add height with trellises, and divide spaces with clipped boxwood hedges. Include an (almost) instant patio by digging away an area of sod and then covering it with a layer of sand and landscaping mesh to discourage weeds. Then cover it with pea gravel, and add a garden bench, statuary, and perhaps an antique or two. The result? European ambiance for even the most nondescript suburban yard.

Plan #F01-351023

Dimensions: 61'8" W x 45'8" D

Levels: 1

Heated Square Footage: 1,600

Bedrooms: 3

Bathrooms: 2

Foundation: Crawl space, slab, or basement

Materials List Available: Yes

Price Category: H

Images provided by designer/architect.

This beautiful three-bedroom home has everything your family needs to live a comfortable life.

Features:

- Great Room: Just off of the foyer you'll discover this large room. It features a cozy fireplace and access to the rear covered porch.

- Dining Room: This formal room has large windows with a view of the backyard.

- Kitchen: This kitchen has an abundance of cabinets and counter space. It is open to the dining room.

- Master Suite: This isolated suite, features a bath with its jetted tub, separate shower, large closet, and a dual sink vanity, is a perfect retreat.

- Bedrooms: The two secondary bedrooms have large closets and share a hall bathroom.

Plan #F01-161007

Dimensions: 66'4" W x 43'10" D

Levels: 1

Heated Square Footage: 1,611

Bedrooms: 3

Bathrooms: 2

Foundation: Basement; crawl space for fee

Materials List Available: Yes

Price Category: C

A lovely front porch and an entry with sidelights invite you to experience the impressive amenities offered in this exceptional ranch home.

Features:

- **Great Room:** Grand openings, featuring columns from the foyer to this great room and continuing to the bayed dining area, convey an open, spacious feel. The fireplace and matching windows on the rear wall of the great room enhance this effect.

- **Kitchen:** This well-designed kitchen offers convenient access to the laundry and garage. It also features an angled counter with ample space and an abundance of cabinets.

- **Master Suite:** This deluxe master suite contains many exciting amenities, including a lavishly appointed dressing room and a large walk-in closet.

- **Porch:** Sliding glass doors lead to this delightful screened porch for relaxing summer interludes.

Images provided by designer/architect.

Rear Elevation

Images provided by designer/architect.

Plan #F01-131001

Dimensions: 72'4" W x 32'4" D
Levels: 1
Heated Square Footage: 1,615
Bedrooms: 3
Bathrooms: 2
Foundation: Crawl space or slab; basement or walkout for fee
Materials List Available: Yes
Price Category: D

Cathedral ceilings and illuminating skylights add drama and beauty to this practical ranch house.

Features:

• Ceiling Height: 8 ft.

• Front Porch: Watch the rain in comfort from the covered front porch.

• Foyer: The stone-tiled foyer flows into the living areas.

• Living Room: Oriented towards the front of the house, the living room opens to the dining room and shares a lovely three-sided fireplace with the family room.

• Family Room: Conveniently located to share the fireplace with the living room, this room is bright and cheery thanks to its skylights as well as the sliding glass doors that open onto the rear patio.

• Kitchen: An island makes this sunny room both efficient and attractive.

Copyright by designer/architect.

• Breakfast Nook: Located just off of the kitchen, this area can serve double-duty as a spot for kitchen visitors to sit.

• Dining Room: The open design between the dining and living rooms adds to the spacious feeling that the cathedral ceiling creates in this area.

• Laundry Room: This area opens from the kitchen for convenience.

• Master Suite: A walk-in closet makes this room practical, but the master bathroom with a skylight, dual-sink vanity, soaking tub, and separate shower makes it luxurious.

• Bedrooms: The two additional bedrooms share a bathroom.

Images provided by designer/architect.

Plan #F01-351033

Dimensions: 64' W x 39' D

Levels: 1

Heated Square Footage: 1,654

Bedrooms: 3

Bathrooms: 2

Foundation: Crawl space, slab, or basement

Materials List Available: Yes

Price Category: H

This gorgeous three-bedroom brick home would be the perfect place to raise your family.

Features:

- Great Room: This terrific room has a gas fireplace with built-in cabinets on both sides.

- Kitchen: This island kitchen with breakfast area is open to the great room.

- Master Suite: This private room features a vaulted ceiling and a large walk-in closet. The bath area has a walk-in closet, jetted tub, and a double-bowl vanity.

- Bedrooms: The two additional bedrooms share a bathroom located in the hall.

CAD FILE AVAILABLE

M. BATH 15' X 10'
3' X 5' JET TUB
3' X 4' SHWR
CLOS. 0'X6'
CLOS. 7'X6'
M. BEDROOM (VAULTED) 14'-6" X 16'
CLOSET
COVERED PORCH 20' X 5'
KITCHEN 12' X 11'
ISLAND
BREAKFAST 11' X 11'
BEDROOM #2 12' X 12'
CLOS.
BATH 8' X 6'
CLOS.
COUNTER
ENTRY
ATTIC ACCESS
2 CAR GARAGE 21' X 23'
UTIL. 8'X8'
GREAT ROOM 23' X 16'
GAS LOGS
CABINETS
HALL
BEDROOM #3 12' X 12'
COVERED PORCH 23' X 4'

Copyright by designer/architect.

Plan #F01-131010

Dimensions: 70' W x 34'4" D
Levels: 1
Heated Square Footage: 1,667
Bedrooms: 3
Bathrooms: 2
Foundation: Crawl space or slab; basement for fee
Materials List Available: Yes
Price Category: D

You'll love this affordable ranch house, with its open floor plan that gives so much usable space, and its graceful layout.

Features:

- **Living Room:** Adjacent to the dining room, this living room features a pass-through fireplace that is open to the family room beyond.

- **Family Room:** A vaulted ceiling with a skylight gives character to this room, where everyone will gather on weekend afternoons and in the evening, to relax.

- **Kitchen:** Also lit from above by a skylight, this kitchen features an island work space.

- **Breakfast Room:** Just off of the kitchen, this breakfast room is sure to be a popular spot at any time of day.

- **Master Bedroom:** Get away from it all in this lovely room, with space to spread out and relax in private.

Laundry Room with Basement

Family Room/Kitchen/Living Room

Plan #F01-241005

Dimensions: 53' W x 55'9" D

Levels: 1

Heated Square Footage: 1,670

Bedrooms: 3

Bathrooms: 2

Foundation: Crawl space or slab; basement for fee

Materials List Available: No

Price Category: C

This charming home with a split-bedroom floor plan, combines big-house features in a compact design.

Features:

- Great Room: With easy access to the formal dining room, kitchen, and breakfast area, this great room features a cozy fireplace.

- Kitchen: This big kitchen, with easy access to a walk-in pantry, features an island for added work space and a lovely plant shelf that separates it from the great room.

- Master Suite: Separated for privacy, this master suite offers a roomy bath with a whirlpool tub, a double-bowl vanity, a separate shower, and a large walk-in closet.

- Additional Rooms: Additional rooms include a laundry/utility room — with space for a washer, dryer, and freezer — a large area above the garage, well-suited for a media or game room, and two secondary bedrooms.

Copyright by designer/architect.

Bonus Area

SMARTtip

Window Scarf

The best way to wrap a window scarf around a pole is as follows:

- Lay out the material on a large, clean surface. Gather the fabric at the top of each jabot, and use elastic to hold it together.

- Swing one jabot into place over the pole and, starting from there, wind the swag portion as many times as you need around the pole until you reach the elastic at the second jabot, which should have landed at the opposite pole end.

- Readjust wraps along the pole. Generally, wrapped swags just touch or slightly overlap.

- For a dramatic effect, stuff the wrapped swags with tissue paper or thin foam, depending on the translucence and weight of fabric.

- Release elastics at tops of jabots.

Plan #F01-241041

Dimensions: 65' W x 45' D

Levels: 1

Heated Square Footage: 1,612

Bedrooms: 3

Bathrooms: 2

Foundation: Slab

Material List Available: No

Price Category: C

Images provided by designer/architect.

Copyright by designer/architect.

Plan #F01-151043

Dimensions: 53' W x 59'10" D

Levels: 1

Heated Square Footage: 1,636

Bedrooms: 3

Bathrooms: 2

Foundation: Crawl space or slab; basement or walkout for fee

Materials List Available: No

Price Category: I

Images provided by designer/architect.

Copyright by designer/architect.

CAD FILE AVAILABLE

Images provided by designer/architect.

CAD FILE AVAILABLE

Plan #F01-351006

Dimensions: 72'10" W x 41' D

Levels: 1

Heated Square Footage: 1,638

Bedrooms: 3

Bathrooms: 2

Foundation: Crawl space, slab, or basement

Materials List Available: Yes

Price Category: H

Stair Location for Basement Option

Plan #F01-391038

Dimensions: 59' W x 44' D

Levels: 1

Heated Square Footage: 1,642

Bedrooms: 3

Bathrooms: 2

Foundation: Crawl space, slab, or basement

Materials List Available: Yes

Price Category: C

Images provided by designer/architect.

CAD FILE AVAILABLE

Optional Basement Stairs

Plan #F01-171006

Dimensions: 68' W x 50' D
Levels: 1
Heated Square Footage: 1,648
Bedrooms: 3
Bathrooms: 2½
Foundation: Crawl space, slab
Materials List Available: Yes
Price Category: C

Images provided by designer/architect.

SMARTtip

Window Shades

While decorative hems add interest to roller shades, they also increase the cost. If you're handy with a glue gun, choose one of the trims available at fabric and craft stores, and consider attaching it yourself. Give your shades fancy pulls for an inexpensive dash of pizzazz.

Plan #F01-121008

Dimensions: 62' W x 56' D
Levels: 1
Heated Square Footage: 1,651
Bedrooms: 2
Bathrooms: 2
Foundation: Basement; crawl space or slab for fee
Materials List Available: Yes
Price Category: C

Images provided by designer/architect.

CAD FILE AVAILABLE

Copyright by designer/architect.

Rear Elevation

Plan #F01-161009

Images provided by designer/architect.

Dimensions: 60'9" W x 49' D

Levels: 1

Heated Square Footage: 1,651

Bedrooms: 3

Bathrooms: 2

Foundation: Basement

Materials List Available: No

Price Category: C

Plan #F01-171008

Images provided by designer/architect.

Dimensions: 72' W x 40' D

Levels: 1

Heated Square Footage: 1,652

Bedrooms: 3

Bathrooms: 2

Foundation: Crawl space or slab

Materials List Available: Yes

Price Category: C

Copyright by designer/architect.

SMARTtip

Lighting for Decorative Shadows

Use lighting to create decorative shadows. For interesting, undefined shadows, set lights at ground level aiming upward in front of a shrub or tree that is close to a wall. For silhouetting, place lights directly behind a plant or garden statue that is near a wall. In both cases, using a wide beam will increase the effect.

1,501–2,500 sq. ft.

Plan #F01-341030

Dimensions: 52' W x 40' D

Levels: 1

Heated Square Footage: 1,660

Bedrooms: 3

Bathrooms: 2

Foundation: Crawl space; slab or basement for fee

Materials List Available: Yes

Price Category: C

Images provided by designer/architect.

CAD FILE AVAILABLE

Copyright by designer/architect.

Plan #F01-761009

Dimensions: 41' W x 60'4" D

Levels: 1

Heated Square Footage: 1,762

Bedrooms: 3

Bathrooms: 2

Foundation: Basement

Materials List Available: Yes

Price Category: C

Images provided by designer/architect.

CAD FILE AVAILABLE

Copyright by designer/architect.

Plan #F01-761012

Dimensions: 60'4" W x 52' D

Levels: 1

Heated Square Footage: 1,820

Bedrooms: 3

Bathrooms: 2

Foundation: Basement

Material List Available: Yes

Price Category: D

Images provided by designer/architect.

CAD FILE AVAILABLE

Copyright by designer/architect.

Br 2 11-8x10-1
Br 3 11-4x10-7
MBr 15-4x16-10 Std Coffer Clg Opt Vaulted Clg
Great Rm 15-9x18-8 Vaulted
Brkfst/Dining 12-0x13-8 Vaulted
Kitchen 19-8x12-8
Workshop/Storage 8-0x13-0
Garage 21-4x22-4
Foyer
Covered Porch
Covered Porch

Plan #F01-341035

Images provided by designer/architect.

CAD FILE AVAILABLE

Dimensions: 60' W x 28' D

Levels: 1

Heated Square Footage: 1,680

Bedrooms: 4

Bathrooms: 2

Foundation: Crawl space; basement or slab for fee

Materials List Available: Yes

Price Category: C

Copyright by designer/architect.

DECK 12'-0" X 10'-0"
GARDEN TUB
BATH 1
CLOSET
KITCHEN 13'-1" X 13'-5" ISLAND
BEDROOM 2 10'-6" X 13'-5"
BATH 2
BEDROOM 3 10'-6" X 10'-11"
BEDROOM 1 13'-11" X 13'-5"
DINING ROOM 12'-4" X 13'-5"
LIVING ROOM 18'-10" X 13'-5"
PREFAB VENTLESS GAS LOG FIREPLACE
BEDROOM 4 10'-6" X 10'-11"
PORCH
28'-0"
60'-0"

Images provided by designer/architect.

Plan #F01-171023

Dimensions: 74' W x 41' D
Levels: 1
Heated Square Footage: 1,684
Bedrooms: 3
Bathrooms: 2
Foundation: Crawl space or slab
Materials List Available: Yes
Price Category: C

This beautifully designed home will be a perfect place to raise your family.

Features:

- Great Room: This large gathering area features a corner fireplace and an 11-ft.-high ceiling. Its direct access to the rear porch enables the room to expand on nice summer days.

- Kitchen: Featuring plenty of workspace and storage, this kitchen is adjacent to the dining room, simplifying mealtime transitions.

- Master Suite: This spacious area features a walk-in closet to simplify the process of getting ready in the morning. The master bath features a stall shower and a garden tub.

- Secondary Bedrooms: Both of the two additional bedrooms have ample closet space and access to a full bathroom.

Plan #F01-131002

Dimensions: 70'1" W x 60'7" D

Levels: 1

Heated Square Footage: 1,709

Bedrooms: 3

Bathrooms: 2½

Foundation: Crawl space or slab; basement or walkout for fee

Materials List Available: Yes

Price Category: D

CAD FILE AVAILABLE

Images provided by designer/architect.

Copyright by designer/architect.

Rear View

You'll love the way this angled ranch brings out the best in a corner lot, or on a slope.

Features:

- Ceiling Height: 8 ft.

- Front Porch: Hang baskets of plants from the roof of this porch, which is just the right size for a couple of rockers and a side table.

- Dining Room: Well-placed windows flood this room with sunlight during the day and a built-in cabinet gives ample storage space for all of your china, linens, and collectables.

- Foyer: Open to the great room, the foyer gives a lovely area to greet your visitors.

- Great Room: A built-in media center surrounds the fireplace where friends and family are sure to gather.

- Master Suite: You'll love the privacy of this somewhat isolated, but easily accessed room. Decorate to show off the large bay window and tray ceiling, and enjoy the luxury of a separate toilet room.

Living Room

Plan #F01-321001

Dimensions: 83' W x 42' D
Levels: 1
Heated Square Footage: 1,721
Bedrooms: 3
Bathrooms: 2
Foundation: Crawl space, slab, or walkout
Materials List Available: Yes
Price Category: E

Images provided by designer/architect.

You'll love the atrium, which creates a warm, naturally lit space inside this gracious home, as well as the roof dormers that give the house wonderful curb appeal from the outside.

Features:

- **Great Room:** Bathed in light from the atrium window wall, this room, with its vaulted ceiling, will be the hub of your family life.

- **Dining Room:** This room also has a vaulted ceiling and is lit by the atrium, but you can draw drapes at night to create a cozy, warm feeling.

- **Kitchen:** Designed for functionality, this step-saving kitchen is easy to organize and makes cooking a pleasure.

- **Breakfast Room:** For convenience, this room is located between the kitchen and the rear covered porch.

- **Master Suite:** Retire with pleasure to this lovely retreat, with its luxurious bath.

Rear View

Front View

Plan #F01-371033

Dimensions: 73' W x 33' 4" D
Levels: 1
Heated Square Footage: 1,724
Bedrooms: 3
Bathrooms: 2
Foundation: Crawl space or slab
Materials List Available: No
Price Category: C

This beautiful brick and stone country home will be the envy of the neighborhood.

Features:

- **Front Porch:** This charming, yet functional porch welcomes you home.

- **Family Room:** This large room, with its cathedral ceiling and cozy fireplace, is ideal for entertaining.

- **Kitchen:** This gourmet kitchen has all the necessities you will ever need, including a raised bar area.

- **Master Suite:** This cozy area features a stepped ceiling. The luxurious bath boasts a marble tub and two walk-in closets.

Copyright by designer/architect.

Images provided by designer/architect.

CAD FILE AVAILABLE

Plan #F01-371011

Dimensions: 55'4" W x 49'10" D

Levels: 1

Heated Square Footage: 1,681

Bedrooms: 3

Bathrooms: 2

Foundation: Crawl space, slab, or basement

Materials List Available: No

Price Category: C

Copyright by designer/architect.

Copyright by designer/architect.

Images provided by designer/architect.

CAD FILE AVAILABLE

Plan #F01-321009

Dimensions: 55'8" W x 46'4" D

Levels: 1

Heated Square Footage: 1,684

Bedrooms: 3

Bathrooms: 2

Foundation: Walkout basement

Materials List Available: Yes

Price Category: E

Rear View

Optional Basement Level

Plan #F01-761045

Dimensions: 56' W x 64'4" D

Levels: 1

Heated Square Footage: 2,050

Bedrooms: 3

Bathrooms: 2

Foundation: Basement

Materials List Available: Yes

Price Category: C

Images provided by designer/architect.

CAD FILE AVAILABLE CAD

Copyright by designer/architect.

Plan drawing labels: Patio; Kit/ Dining 17-4x19-7 Tray Clg; MBr 17-4x14-8 Std Vault Clg Opt Coffer Clg; Great Rm 20-1x19-8 Vault Clg; Laundry; Br 2 12-2x11-4; Br 3 11-10x11-4; Foyer; Garage 23-4x25-8; Porch

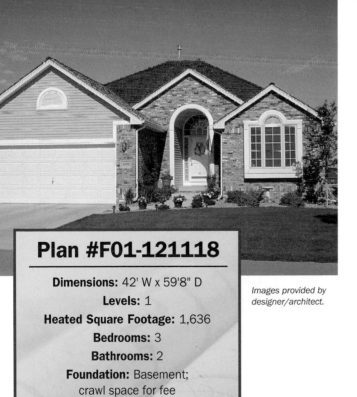

Plan #F01-121118

Dimensions: 42' W x 59'8" D

Levels: 1

Heated Square Footage: 1,636

Bedrooms: 3

Bathrooms: 2

Foundation: Basement; crawl space for fee

Materials List Available: Yes

Price Category: C

Images provided by designer/architect.

Bfst. 12⁰ x 12⁰; Grt. rm. 14⁰ x 20⁰ 10'-0" CEILING; Mbr. 14' x 14' 9'-0" CEILING; Kit. 12⁰ x 13⁰; Din. 13⁴ x 11⁰ 10'-0" CEILING; Br. 3 11³ x 10⁰ OPTIONAL DEN; Gar. 19³ x 21⁴; Br. 2 11³ x 10⁰ 9'-4" CEILING; TRANSOMS; SKYLIGHT; WHIRLPOOL; DESK; SNACK BAR; PANT.; HUTCH; WORK BENCH; CVRD. STOOP; 59'-8"; 42'-0"

Copyright by designer/architect.

Porch
12' x 12'

Master Bedroom
15' x 13'2"

TRAY CEILING

WALK-IN CLOSET

Bath

Great Room- Dining
28'8" x 16'11" Irr.

STEPPED CEILING

Kitchen
12' x 12' Irr.

Laun.
7'4" x 6'

PANTRY

DOWN

Hall

Bath

Bedroom
11'4" x 12'

Bedroom/
Den
10'2" x 11'6"

Foyer

Porch

Two-Car Garage
20' x 21'

Images provided by designer/architect.

Copyright by designer/architect.

Plan #F01-161014

Dimensions: 51'8" W x 49'8" D
Levels: 1
Heated Square Footage: 1,698
Bedrooms: 3
Bathrooms: 2
Foundation: Basement; slab for fee
Materials List Available: Yes
Price Category: C

Rear Elevation

Plan #F01-321026

Dimensions: 67' W x 42'4" D
Levels: 1
Heated Square Footage: 1,712
Bedrooms: 3
Bathrooms: 2½
Foundation: Crawl space
Materials List Available: Yes
Price Category: C

Images provided by designer/architect.

CAD FILE AVAILABLE

67'-0"

Patio

Copyright by designer/architect.

Sunken

Great Rm
18-0x18-0

Dining
12-0x14-8

Br 3
12-7x12-0

MBr
15-0x12-0

Kit

R

P

W D

Entry

Garage
20-4x20-8

L

Br 2
12-4x12-0

Porch depth 5-0

42'-4"

SMARTtip

Deck Design with Computers

Consider using a computer-aided design (CAD) program to plan your deck. Some programs let you see three-dimensional views of your design complete with railings, stairs, planters, hot tubs, and the surrounding landscaping.

Plan #F01-341029

Dimensions: 49' W x 57' D

Levels: 1

Heated Square Footage: 1,737

Bedrooms: 3

Bathrooms: 2

Foundation: Crawl space; slab or basement for fee

Materials List Available: Yes

Price Category: C

Images provided by designer/architect.

CAD FILE AVAILABLE

Plan #F01-391034

Dimensions: 72'4" W x 43' D

Levels: 1

Heated Square Footage: 1,737

Bedrooms: 3

Bathrooms: 2

Foundation: Crawl space, slab, or basement

Materials List Available: Yes

Price Category: C

Images provided by designer/architect.

This home, as shown in the photograph, may differ from the actual blueprints. For more detailed information, please check the floor plans carefully.

Rear View

Copyright by designer/architect.

www.ultimateplans.com   95

Images provided by designer/architect.

Plan #F01-441004

Dimensions: 55' W x 48' D

Levels: 1

Heated Square Footage: 1,728

Bedrooms: 2

Bathrooms: 2

Foundation: Crawl space; slab or basement available for fee

Materials List Available: No

Price Category: E

Empty nesters and first-time homeowners will adore the comfort within this charming home. Rooms benefit from the many windows, which welcome light into the home.

Features:

- Great Room: This vaulted room is equipped with a built-in media center and fireplace. Windows span across the back of the room and the adjoining dining room, extending the perceived area and offering access to the covered patio.

- Kitchen: Taking advantage of corner space, this kitchen provides ample cabinets and countertops to store goods and prepare meals. Every chef will appreciate the extra space afforded by the pantry.

- Master Suite: This luxurious escape has a large sleeping area with views of the backyard. The master bath features a spa tub, a double-bowl vanity and a walk-in closet.

- Garage: This front-loading two-car garage has a shop area located in the rear.

Rear Elevation

Images provided by designer/architect.

Plan #F01-151173

Dimensions: 58' W x 53'6" D
Levels: 1
Heated Square Footage: 1,739
Bedrooms: 3
Bathrooms: 2
Foundation: Crawl space or slab; basement or walkout for fee
Materials List Available: No
Price Category: I

You'll love the charming architectural features and practical contemporary design of this ranch-style home.

Features:

- Great Room: Perfect for entertaining guests or just cozying up to the glowing fireplace, this great room is conveniently located in the center of everything.

- Kitchen: This highly efficient design, complete with island and plenty of workspace and storage, is just steps away from the sunlit breakfast room and the formal dining room, simplifying meal transitions.

- Master Suite: A romantic getaway in itself, this spacious master bedroom adjoins double walk-in closets, and a large compartmentalized master bath with a whirlpool tub, a double-bowl vanity and a standing shower. The room also includes a private entrance to the back porch.

- Secondary Bedrooms: These two nicely sized bedrooms share access to a full bathroom.

Plan #F01-321008

Dimensions: 57' W x 52'2" D

Levels: 1

Heated Square Footage: 1,761

Bedrooms: 4

Bathrooms: 2

Foundation: Basement

Materials List Available: Yes

Price Category: C

One look at the roof dormers and planter boxes that grace the outside of this ranch, and you'll know that the interior is planned for comfortable family living.

Features:

- Great Room: A vaulted ceiling in this room points up its generous dimensions. Put a grouping of relaxing chairs near the fireplace to take advantage of the cozy spot it creates in chilly weather.

- Kitchen: Open to the great room, this kitchen has been planned for convenience. It features a pass-through to the dining area for easy serving when you've got a crowd to feed.

- Master Bedroom: A vaulted ceiling makes you feel especially pampered, and the walk-in closet and bath with tub, shower and double vanity add to that feeling.

- Additional Bedrooms: Great closet space characterizes all of the rooms in this home, making it easy for children of any age to keep it organized and tidy.

Images provided by designer/architect.

Copyright by designer/architect.

SMARTtip

Hanging Wallpaper

Use liner paper to smooth out a damaged wall and to provide uniform support for expensive paper.

Plan #F01-151009

Dimensions: 44' W x 86'2" D
Levels: 1
Heated Square Footage: 1,601
Bedrooms: 3
Bathrooms: 2
Foundation: Crawl space or slab
Materials List Available: No
Price Category: H

Images provided by designer/architect.

This can be the perfect home for a site with views you can enjoy in all seasons and at all times.

Features:

- **Porches:** Enjoy the front porch with its 10-ft. ceiling and the more private back porch where you can set up a grill or just get away from it all.

- **Foyer:** With a 10-ft. ceiling, this foyer opens to the great room for a warm welcome.

- **Great Room:** Your family will love the media center and the easy access to the rear porch.

- **Kitchen:** This well-designed kitchen is open to the dining room and the breakfast nook, which also opens to the rear covered porch.

- **Master Suite:** The bedroom has a 10-ft. boxed ceiling and a door to the rear. The bath includes a corner whirlpool tub with glass block windows.

- **Bedrooms:** Bedroom 2 has a vaulted ceiling, while bedroom 3 features a built-in desk.

Plan #F01-351002

Dimensions: 64' W x 45'10" D
Levels: 1
Heated Square Footage: 1,751
Bedrooms: 3
Bathrooms: 2
Foundation: Crawl space, slab, or basement
Materials List Available: Yes
Price Category: H

Images provided by designer/architect.

This is a beautiful classic traditional home with a European touch.

Features:

- Great Room: This gathering area has a gas log fireplace that is flanked by two built-in cabinets. The area has a 10-ft.-tall tray ceiling.

- Kitchen: This L-shaped island kitchen has a raised bar and is open to the eating area and great room. The three open spaces work together as one large room.

- Master Suite: Located on the opposite side of the home from the secondary bedrooms, this suite has a vaulted ceiling. The master bath has a double-bowl vanity and a garden tub.

- Bedrooms: The two secondary bedrooms share a hall bathroom and have ample closet space.

Great Room

Kitchen

Master Bathroom

Garden Tub

M. Bath
15-0 x 10-0

Master Bedroom
14-6 x 16-0

VAULT

VAULT

Covered Porch
23-0 x 5-0

Bedroom 2
12-0 x 12-0
9-0 Ceiling

Kitchen
12-0 x 11-0

Island

Eating
11-0 x 11-0
9-0 Ceiling

BAR

C
8-0 x 6-0

C
7-0 x 6-0

F **Utility**
9-6 x 8-0

Entry

Stor.
8-0 x 7-0

D W

C

Media/Hobby
9-0 x 8-0

Trayed Ceiling

9-0 Ceiling

10-0 Ceiling

Great Room
23-0 x 16-0

Cabs

Hall

Hall Bath

Tub/ Shr.

Lin.

C

Gas Logs

Cabs

Bedroom 3
12-0 x 12-0
9-0 Ceiling

OPTIONAL STAIRS TO BASEMENT

NOTE: ALL DASHED WALLS INDICATE OPTIONAL WALL LOCATIONS IF BASEMENT OPTION IS CHOSEN.

2 Car Garage
21-0 x 22-0

Copyright by designer/architect.

(OPTIONAL GARAGE EXTENSION NOT INCLUDED IN OVERALL DIMENSIONS)

OPTIONAL EXTENSION OF GARAGE IF BASEMENT OPTION IS CHOSEN.

Covered Porch
23-0 x 4-0

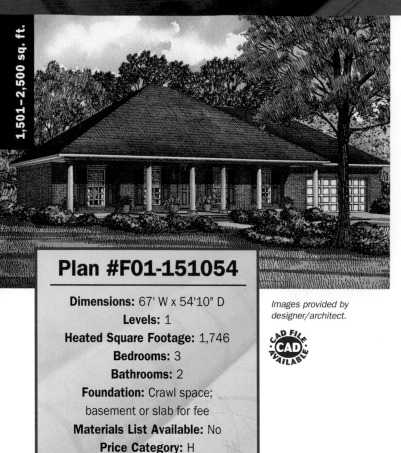

Plan #F01-151054

Dimensions: 67' W x 54'10" D

Levels: 1

Heated Square Footage: 1,746

Bedrooms: 3

Bathrooms: 2

Foundation: Crawl space; basement or slab for fee

Materials List Available: No

Price Category: H

Images provided by designer/architect.

CAD FILE AVAILABLE

SMARTtip

Mixing and Matching Windows

Windows, both fixed and operable, are made in various styles and shapes. While mixing styles should be carefully avoided, a variety of interesting window sizes and shapes may nevertheless be combined to achieve symmetry, harmony, and rhythm on the exterior of a home.

Plan #F01-221011

Dimensions: 59' W x 58' D

Levels: 1

Heated Square Footage: 1,756

Bedrooms: 3

Bathrooms: 2

Foundation: Basement

Materials List Available: No

Price Category: C

Images provided by designer/architect.

CAD FILE AVAILABLE

Rear Elevation

Plan #F01-121331

Dimensions: 62' W x 48' D

Levels: 1

Heated Square Footage: 1,763

Bedrooms: 3

Bathrooms: 2½

Foundation: Basement

Materials List Available: Yes

Price Category: G

Images provided by designer/architect.

CAD FILE AVAILABLE

Plan #F01-171009

Dimensions: 68' W x 50' D

Levels: 1

Heated Square Footage: 1,771

Bedrooms: 3

Bathrooms: 2

Foundation: Crawl space or slab

Materials List Available: No

Price Category: C

Images provided by designer/architect.

SMARTtip

Deck Awnings

Awnings come in bright colors. As light filters through, it will cast a hue to anything under the deck. Warm colors, such as red or pink, will create a rosy glow; cool colors, such blues or greens, will enhance the shade.

Plan #F01-191003

Dimensions: 56' W x 42' D

Levels: 1

Heated Square Footage: 1,785

Bedrooms: 3

Bathrooms: 3

Foundation: Crawl space, slab, or basement

Materials List Available: No

Price Category: E

Images provided by designer/architect.

Copyright by designer/architect.

Plan #F01-271077

Dimensions: 69'6" W x 53' D

Levels: 1

Heated Square Footage: 1,786

Bedrooms: 1

Bathrooms: 1½

Foundation: Basement or walkout

Materials List Available: No

Price Category: C

Images provided by designer/architect.

CAD FILE AVAILABLE

Copyright by designer/architect.

Optional Basement Level

Copyright by designer/architect.

Plan #F01-321010

Dimensions: 59' W x 37'8" D
Levels: 1
Heated Square Footage: 1,787
Bedrooms: 3
Bathrooms: 2
Foundation: Basement or walkout
Materials List Available: Yes
Price Category: C

Images provided by designer/architect.

CAD FILE AVAILABLE

Plan #F01-211002

Dimensions: 68' W x 62' D
Levels: 1
Heeated Square Footage: 1,792
Bedrooms: 3
Bathrooms: 2
Foundation: Crawl space; basement or slab for fee
Materials List Available: Yes
Price Category: C

Images provided by designer/architect.

Plan #F01-351003

Dimensions: 64' W x 45'10" D

Levels: 1

Heated Square Footage: 1,751

Bedrooms: 3

Bathrooms: 2

Foundation: Crawl space, slab, or basement

Materials List Available: Yes

Price Category: H

This beautiful three-bedroom brick house with a covered porch is perfect for today's families.

Features:

- **Great Room:** This gathering room features a tray ceiling, a gas fireplace, and built-in cabinets.

- **Kitchen:** This island kitchen with a raised bar is open to the great room and eating area.

- **Master Suite:** This primary bedroom features a vaulted ceiling and large walk-in closet. The private bath boasts a double-bowl vanity, a corner tub, and a walk-in closet.

- **Bedrooms:** Two additional bedrooms are located on the other side of the home from the master suite and share a common bathroom.

Images provided by designer/architect.

CAD FILE AVAILABLE

Garden Tub

M. Bath 15-0 x 10-0

S

C 8-0 x 6-0

C 7-0 x 6-0

Master Bedroom 14-6 x 16-0

VAULT

VAULT

Stor. 8-0 x 7-0

Utility 9-6 x 8-0

F

D W

Entry

C

Covered Porch 23-0 x 5-0

Kitchen 12-0 x 11-0

Island

DW

P

BAR

Eating 11-0 x 11-0
9-0 Ceiling

Bedroom 2 12-0 x 12-0
9-0 Ceiling

Brm

C

Hall Bath
Tub/ Shr.

Hall

Lin.

C

Media/ Hobby 9-0 x 8-0

Trayed Ceiling

9-0 Ceiling

10-0 Ceiling

Great Room 23-0 x 16-0

Cabs

Gas Logs

Cabs

Bedroom 3 12-0 x 12-0
9-0 Ceiling

Covered Porch 23-0 x 4-0

NOTE: ALL DASHED WALLS INDICATE OPTIONAL WALL LOCATIONS IF BASEMENT OPTION IS CHOSEN.

OPTIONAL STAIRS TO BASEMENT

2 Car Garage 21-0 x 22-0

Copyright by designer/architect.

(OPTIONAL GARAGE EXTENSION NOT INCLUDED IN OVERALL DIMENSIONS)

OPTIONAL EXTENSION OF GARAGE IF BASEMENT OPTION IS CHOSEN.

Front View

Dining Room

Kitchen

Great Room

Master Bathroom

Rear View

Images provided by designer/architect.

Plan #F01-161001

Dimensions: 67'2" W x 47' D

Levels: 1

Heated Square Footage: 1,782

Bedrooms: 3

Bathrooms: 2

Foundation: Basement; slab for fee

Materials List Available: No

Price Category: C

An all-brick exterior displays the solid strength that characterizes this gracious home.

Features:

- Great Room: A feeling of spaciousness permeates the gathering area created by the foyer, great room, and dining room. Multiple windows provide natural light that dances along a sloped ceiling, spilling onto decorative columns and a fireplace.

- Breakfast Area: A continuation of the sloped ceiling leads to the breakfast area where French doors open to a screened porch.

- Kitchen: An abundance of cabinets and counter space are the hallmarks of this large kitchen with its easy access to a spacious laundry room and storage area.

- Master Suite: A stepped-up tray ceiling and spacious walk-in closet in the master bedroom, along with a whirlpool tub, and double-bowl vanity in the bathroom, enable you to pamper yourself.

Great Room/Foyer

Rear Elevation

Plan #F01-101004

Dimensions: 55'8" W x 56'6" D

Levels: 1

Heated Square Footage: 1,787

Bedrooms: 3

Bathrooms: 2

Foundation: Crawl space, slab, basement, or walkout

Materials List Available: Yes

Price Category: F

This carefully designed ranch provides the feel and features of a much larger home.

Features:

- Ceiling Height: 9 ft. unless otherwise noted.

- Entry: Guests will step up onto the inviting covered front porch and into this entry, with its impressive 11-ft. ceiling.

- Dining Room: Open to the entry and to the left is the elegant dining room, perfect for entertaining or informal family gatherings.

- Family Room: This family gathering place features an 11-ft. ceiling to enhance its sense of spaciousness.

- Kitchen: This intelligently designed kitchen has an open plan. A breakfast bar and a serving bar are features that add to its convenience.

- Master Suite: This suite is loaded with amenities, including a double-step tray ceiling, direct access to the screened porch, a sitting room, deluxe bath, and double walk-in closets.

Images provided by designer/architect.

Plan #F01-151007

Dimensions: 54'2" W x 56'2" D

Levels: 1

Heated Square Footage: 1,787

Bedrooms: 3

Bathrooms: 2

Foundation: Crawl space or slab; basement or walkout for fee

Materials List Available: No

Price Category: H

Images provided by designer/architect.

This home, as shown in the photograph, may differ from the actual blueprints. For more detailed information, please check the floor plans carefully.

This compact, well-designed home is graced with amenities usually reserved for larger houses.

Features:

• Foyer: A 10-ft. ceiling creates unity between the foyer and the dining room just beyond it.

• Dining Room: 8-in. boxed columns welcome you into this dining room, with its 10-ft. ceilings.

• Great Room: The 9-ft. boxed ceiling suits the spacious design in this large room. Enjoy the fireplace in the winter and the rear-grilling porch in the summer.

• Breakfast Room: This bright room is a lovely spot for any time of day.

• Master Suite: A double vanity and a large walk-in closet add practicality to this quiet room with a 9-ft. pan ceiling. The master bath includes a whirlpool tub with glass blocks and a separate shower.

• Bedrooms: Bedroom 2 features a bay window, and both rooms are close to the bathroom.

Plan #F01-321003

Dimensions: 67'4" W x 48' D

Levels: 1

Heated Square Footage: 1,791

Bedrooms: 4

Bathrooms: 2

Foundation: Basement

Materials List Available: Yes

Price Category: E

The traditional good looks of the exterior of this home are complemented by the stunning contemporary design of the interior.

Features:

- Great Room: With a vaulted ceiling to highlight its spacious dimensions, this room is certain to be the central gathering spot for friends and family.

- Dining Room: Also with a vaulted ceiling, this room has an octagon shape for added interest. Windows here and in the great room look out to the covered patio.

- Kitchen: A center island gives a convenient work space in this well-designed kitchen, which features a pass-through to the dining room for easy serving, and large, walk-in pantry for storage.

- Breakfast Room: A bay window lets sunshine pour in to start your morning with a smile.

- Master Bedroom: A vaulted ceiling and a sitting area make you feel truly pampered in this room.

SMARTtip

Bay & Bow Windows

Occasionally too little room exists between the window frame (if there is one) and the ceiling. In this situation you might be able to use ceiling-mounted hardware. Alternatively, a cornice across the top and a rod mounted inside the cornice will give you the dual benefit of visually lowering the top of the window and concealing the hardware.

Plan #F01-391019

Dimensions: 56' W x 32' D
Levels: 1
Heated Square Footage: 1,792
Bedrooms: 3
Bathrooms: 2
Foundation: Walkout basement
Materials List Available: No
Price Category: C

Images provided by designer/architect.

This southern-style cottage with sociable porch fits in almost anywhere, from a leafy lane to hillside or curbside and renders a lot of living space and hospitality.

Features:

• Family Room: This room features a central stone fireplace, plus two walls of windows to usher in the light. Sloping ceilings and decorative beams boost its rustic charm. An enormously generous space, it opens wide to the corner kitchen.

• Dining Room: This room has its own level of sophistication, including entry outside to the deck and spacious atmosphere.

• Laundry Area: The family-sized pantry and laundry area are set off by themselves to avoid interference with everyday living.

• Master Suite: A leisurely hall leads to the master bedroom and private full bath, wide walk-in closets, and a trio of windows.

• Bedrooms: Across the hall the two secondary bedrooms share a roomy bath and a view of the front porch.

Front View

Side/Rear View

Copyright by designer/architect.

MAIN AREA

Plan #F01-431001

Dimensions: 58'8" W x 62' D

Levels: 1

Heated Square Footage: 1,792

Bedrooms: 3

Bathrooms: 2½

Foundation: Crawl space or basement

Materials List Available: Yes

Price Category: C

Your neighbors will envy this Southern-style home.

Features:

- **Great Room:** The entry overlooks this room, where a fireplace warms gatherings on chilly evenings. A large window and French doors allow a view of the yard.

- **Kitchen:** The primary workstation in this kitchen is a peninsula, which faces the fireplace in the great room. The peninsula is equipped with a sink and snack counter.

- **Master Suite:** This private space is located on the other side of the home from the other bedrooms. It contains expansive double walk-in closets, a spa tub, and a double-bowl vanity.

- **Bedrooms:** Two additional bedrooms are separated from the master suite. Both bedrooms have large closets and share a hall bathroom.

Copyright by designer/architect.

Rear Elevation

Plan #F01-131047

Dimensions: 69'10" W x 51'8" D

Levels: 1

Heated Square Footage: 1,793

Bedrooms: 3

Bathrooms: 2

Foundation: Crawl space or slab; basement for fee

Materials List Available: Yes

Price Category: D

Images provided by designer/architect.

The country charm of this well-designed home is mixed with the convenience and luxury normally reserved for more contemporary plans.

Features:

- Great Room: The spaciousness of this great room is enhanced by the 11-ft. stepped ceiling. A fireplace makes it cozy on cool evenings, or on chilly winter days, and two sets of French sliding glass doors open to the back porch.

- Kitchen: In addition to the convenient layout of this design, you'll also love its bright, airy position. It includes an old-fashioned pantry, a sink under a window, and a sunny breakfast area that opens to the wraparound porch.

- Master Suite: You'll find 11-ft. ceilings in both the master bedroom and the bayed sitting area that the suite includes. In the bath, the circular spa tub is surrounded by a glass-block wall.

- Bonus Space: A permanent staircase leads to an unfinished bonus space on the upper level.

Copyright by designer/architect.

Bonus Area

Rear View

Images provided by designer/architect.

Plan #F01-151196

Dimensions: 89' W x 49'4" D
Levels: 1
Heated Square Footage: 1,800
Bedrooms: 3
Bathrooms: 2
Foundation: Crawl space or slab; basement for fee
Materials List Available: No
Price Category: H

This charming home, with its wide front porch, is perfect on a little piece of land, or a quiet suburban street.

Features:

- **Screened Porch:** This screened porch creates extra living space where you can enjoy warm summer breezes in a bug-free atmosphere.

- **Great Room:** Make a "great" first impression by welcoming guests into this spacious, firelight-illuminated great room.

- **Kitchen:** This efficient area is surrounded on all sides by workspace and storage. A snack bar, adjacent dining room, and attached grilling porch create plenty of mealtime options.

- **Master Suite:** This master suite creates a stress-free environment with its large walk-in closet, whirlpool tub, standing shower, and double vanities.

Copyright by designer/architect.

Plan #F01-441005

Dimensions: 50' W x 59' D

Levels: 1

Heated Square Footage: 1,800

Bedrooms: 3

Bathrooms: 2

Foundation: Crawl space; slab or basement for fee

Materials List Available: No

Price Category: E

Images provided by designer/architect.

This home looks as if it's a quaint little abode - with its board-and-batten siding, cedar shingle detailing, and column-covered porch - but even a quick peek inside will prove that there is much more to this plan than meets the eye.

Features:

• Foyer: This entry area rises to a 9-ft.-high ceiling. On one side is a washer-dryer alcove with a closet across the way; on the other is another large storage area. Just down the hallway is a third closet.

• Bedrooms: Three bedrooms (or two plus an office) are found on the right side of the plan.

• Kitchen: This kitchen features a center island, built-in desk/work center, and pantry. This area and the dining area also boast 9-ft.-high ceilings and are open to a vaulted great room with corner fireplace.

• Dining Room: Sliding glass doors in this area lead to a covered side porch to enjoy outside dining.

• Master Suite: This suite has a vaulted ceiling. The master bath is wonderfully appointed with a separate shower, spa tub, and dual sinks.

Rear Elevation

59'

50'

Copyright by designer/architect.

Plan #F01-161002

Dimensions: 64'2" W x 44'2" D
Levels: 1
Heated Square Footage: 1,860
Bedrooms: 3
Bathrooms: 2
Foundation: Basement
Materials List Available: Yes
Price Category: D

Images provided by designer/architect.

The brick, stone, and cedar shake facade provides color and texture to the exterior, while the unique nooks and angles inside this delightful one-level home give it character.

Features:

- Great Room/Dining Room: This spacious great room is furnished with a wood-burning fireplace, a high ceiling, and French doors. Wide entrances to the breakfast room and dining room expand its space to comfortably hold large gatherings.

- Kitchen: The breakfast bar offers additional seating. The covered porch lets you enjoy a view of the landscape and is conveniently located for outdoor meals off this kitchen and breakfast area.

- Master Suite: The master suite is a private retreat. An alcove creates a comfortable sitting area, and an angled entry leads to the bath with whirlpool and a double-bowl vanity.

Great Room/Foyer

Rear Elevation

Copyright by designer/architect.

Plan #F01-221009

Dimensions: 68' W x 59' D

Levels: 1

Heated Square Footage: 1,795

Bedrooms: 3

Bathrooms: 2

Foundation: Basement

Materials List Available: No

Price Category: C

Images provided by designer/architect.

CAD FILE AVAILABLE

Rear Elevation

Plan #F01-371104

Dimensions: 57' W x 52'6" D

Levels: 1

Heated Square Footage: 1,795

Bedrooms: 3

Bathrooms: 2

Foundation: Crawl space or slab

Materials List Available: No

Price Category: C

Images provided by designer/architect.

Plan #F01-351038

Dimensions: 65' W x 50' D

Levels: 1

Heated Square Footage: 1,800

Bedrooms: 3

Bathrooms: 2

Foundation: Crawl space, slab, or basement

Materials List Available: Yes

Price Category: H

Images provided by designer/architect.

Copyright by designer/architect.

Plan #F01-151656

Dimensions: 43'8" W x 71'6" D

Levels: 1

Heated Square Footage: 1,806

Bedrooms: 3

Bathrooms: 2

Foundation: Crawl space or slab; basement or walkout for fee

Materials List Available: No

Price Category: H

Images provided by designer/architect.

Copyright by designer/architect.

Rear Elevation

Plan #F01-221099

Images provided by designer/architect.

CAD FILE AVAILABLE

Dimensions: 63' W x 53' D

Levels: 1

Heated Square Footage: 1,829

Bedrooms: 2

Bathrooms: 2

Foundation: Basement

Materials List Available: Yes

Price Category: D

Plan #F01-761008

Images provided by designer/architect.

CAD FILE AVAILABLE

Dimensions: 65' W x 46'4" D

Levels: 1

Heated Square Footage: 1,562

Bedrooms: 3

Bathrooms: 2

Foundation: Basement

Materials List Available: Yes

Price Category: C

Rear Elevation

Plan #F01-251006

Dimensions: 65'5" W x 59'11" D

Levels: 1

Heated Square Footage: 1,849

Bedrooms: 3

Bathrooms: 2

Foundation: Crawl space or slab

Materials List Available: Yes

Price Category: D

Images provided by designer/architect.

Copyright by designer/architect.

Plan #F01-441001

Dimensions: 44' W x 68' D

Levels: 1

Heated Square Footage: 1,850

Bedrooms: 3

Bathrooms: 2

Foundation: Crawl space; slab or basement for fee

Materials List Available: No

Price Category: E

Images provided by designer/architect.

Rear Elevation

Copyright by designer/architect.

Plan #F01-351001

Dimensions: 72'8" W x 51' D

Levels: 1

Heated Square Footage: 1,855

Bedrooms: 3

Bathrooms: 2½

Foundation: Crawl space, slab, or basement

Materials List Available: Yes

Price Category: H

Images provided by designer/architect.

From the lovely arched windows on the front to the front and back covered porches, this home is as comfortable as it is beautiful.

Features:

• Great Room: Enter this room with 12-ft. ceilings, and you're sure to admire the corner gas fireplace and three windows overlooking the porch.

• Dining Room: Set off from the open design, this room is designed to be used formally or not.

• Kitchen: You'll love the practical walk-in pantry, broom closet, and angled snack bar here.

• Breakfast Room: Brightly lit and leading to the covered porch, this room will be a favorite spot.

• Bonus Room: Add on a playroom, study, or home gym in this area.

• Master Suite: The bedroom is complemented by the private bath with garden tub, separate shower, double vanity, and spacious walk-in closet.

Kitchen

Bonus Area Floor Plan

Plan #F01-131015

Dimensions: 57'4" W x 56'10" D

Levels: 1

Heated Square Footage: 1,860

Bedrooms: 3

Bathrooms: 2

Foundation: Crawl space or slab; basement for fee

Materials List Available: Yes

Price Category: E

This home, as shown in the photograph, may differ from the actual blueprints. For more detailed information, please check the floor plans carefully

The mixture of country charm and formal elegance is sure to thrill any family looking for a distinctive and comfortable home.

Features:

- Great Room: Separated from the dining room by a columned arch, this spacious room has a stepped ceiling, a built-in media center, and a fireplace. French doors in a rear bay lead to the large backyard patio at the rear of the house.

Images provided by designer/architect.

- Dining Room: Graced by a bay window, this formal room has an impressive 11-ft. 6-in.-high stepped ceiling.

- Breakfast Room: With a 12-ft. sloped ceiling, this room shares an eating bar with the kitchen.

- Master Bedroom: The 10-ft. tray ceiling and bay window add elegance, and the walk-in closet and bath with a bayed nook, whirlpool tub, and separate shower make it practical.

Rear Elevation

Great Room

Plan #F01-161073

Dimensions: 66' W x 69' D

Levels: 1

Heated Square Footage: 1,895

Bedrooms: 3

Bathrooms: 2

Foundation: Basement; slab or crawl space for fee

Materials List Available: No

Price Category: D

Images provided by designer/architect.

The brick exterior with quoins, arched windows, and wood trim creates a rich, solid look in this delightful one-level home.

Features:

- **Great Room:** This large gathering area is decorated by a gas fireplace and offers a view of the rear yard.

- **Dining Room:** This open room is topped with a sloped ceiling that reaches 12-ft. high.

- **Kitchen:** This large kitchen, with its angled snack bar, and the breakfast area both open generously to the great room for a continuous traffic flow.

- **Master Suite:** This luxurious suite enjoys a corner whirlpool tub, double-bowl vanity, private toilet closet, walk-in closet and private shower enclosure.

Rear Elevation

Right Elevation

Left Elevation

Plan #F01-441002

Dimensions: 70' W x 51' D

Levels: 1

Heated Square Footage: 1,873

Bedrooms: 3

Bathrooms: 2

Foundation: Crawl space; basement or slab for fee

Materials List Available: No

Price Category: E

Images provided by designer/architect.

Shutters flank tall windows to adorn the front of this charming home. A high roofline gives presence to the facade and allows vaulted ceilings in all the right places inside.

Features:

- **Great Room:** The entry hall overlooks this room, where a fireplace warms gatherings on chilly evenings and built-in shelves, to the right of the fireplace, add space that might be used as an entertainment center. A large three-panel window wall allows for a rear-yard view.

- **Dining Room:** This area is connected directly to the great room and features double doors to a covered porch.

- **Kitchen:** This open work area contains ample counter space with an island cooktop and large pantry.

- **Bedrooms:** The bedrooms are split, with the master suite in the back and additional bedrooms at the front.

- **Master Suite:** This suite boasts a 9-ft.-high ceiling and is graced by a luxurious bathroom and a walk-in closet.

Rear Elevation

1,501–2,500 sq. ft.

Rear Elevation

Plan #F01-221005

Images provided by designer/architect.

 CAD FILE AVAILABLE

Dimensions: 72' W x 42' D
Levels: 1
Heated Square Footage: 1,851
Bedrooms: 3
Bathrooms: 2
Foundation: Basement
Materials List Available: No
Price Category: D

Copyright by designer/architect.

Plan #F01-351004

CAD FILE AVAILABLE

Images provided by designer/architect.

Dimensions: 78' W x 49'6" D
Levels: 1
Heated Square Footage: 1,852
Bedrooms: 3
Bathrooms: 2½
Foundation: Crawl space, slab, or basement
Materials List Available: Yes
Price Category: H

Bonus Room

Rear View

Bonus Room

Plan #F01-151233

Dimensions: 90' W x 49'4" D

Levels: 1

Heated Square Footage: 1,853

Bedrooms: 3

Bathrooms: 2

Foundation: Crawl space or slab; basement or walkout for fee

Materials List Available: No

Price Category: H

Images provided by designer/architect.

CAD FILE AVAILABLE

Kitchen

Copyright by designer/architect.

Plan #F01-191004

Dimensions: 58' W x 68' D

Levels: 1

Heated Square Footage: 1,856

Bedrooms: 3

Bathrooms: 3

Foundation: Crawl space or slab

Materials List Available: No

Price Category: E

Images provided by designer/architect.

Plan #F01-211039

Dimensions: 62' W x 64' D

Levels: 1

Heated Square Footage: 1,868

Bedrooms: 3

Bathrooms: 2

Foundation: Slab; crawl space for fee

Materials List Available: Yes

Price Category: D

Images provided by designer/architect.

Plan #F01-151068

Dimensions: 57' W x 61'4" D

Levels: 1

Heated Square Footage: 1,880

Bedrooms: 4

Bathrooms: 2

Foundation: Crawl space or slab; basement or walkout for fee

Materials List Available: No

Price Category: I

Images provided by designer/architect.

GARAGE
23 x 31

PORCH

wh
w
d
H
P

BEDROOM
10 x 15

BEDROOM
10 x 15

BEDROOM
16 x 16

loft over

pass-thru

KIT.
16 x 13

LIV. / DINING
19 x 25

PORCH

Copyright by designer/architect.

Images provided by designer/architect.

Plan #F01-381010

Dimensions: 62' W x 87'6" D

Levels: 1

Heated Square Footage: 1,905

Bedrooms: 3

Bathrooms: 2

Foundation: Crawl space

Materials List Available: Yes

Price Category: E

Copyright by designer/architect.

56'-0"

64'-4"

SCREENED PORCH
16'-0" X 12'-0"

BREAKFAST ROOM
10'-0" X 10'-7"

MASTER SUITE
10' BOXED CEILING
14'-0" X 15'-6"

REF.

KITCHEN
10'-0" X 11'-8"

RG
DW
PAN

GREAT RM.
16'-0" X 20'-8"

BEDROOM 3
12'-0" X 11'-6"

LIN.
LIN.

GLASS BLOCKS

WHP TUB

VAULTED CEILING

W.I.C.
11'-8" X 5'-6"

W
D

8" COLUMNS

FOYER
10' CEILING
7'-0" X 7'-10"

DINING RM.
10' CEILING
12'-2" X 11'-4"

BEDROOM 2
12'-0" X 11'-10"

OPTIONAL VAULTED CEILING

STRG.

DN

TO OPTIONAL BASEMENT

PORCH
7'-6" X 5'-2"

GARAGE
22'-10" X 20'-8"

Plan #F01-151075

Dimensions: 56' W x 64'4" D

Levels: 1

Heated Square Footage: 1,909

Bedrooms: 3

Bathrooms: 2

Foundation: Crawl space or slab; basement for fee

Materials List Available: No

Price Category: H

Images provided by designer/architect.

CAD FILE AVAILABLE

Plan #F01-441006

Dimensions: 48' W x 64' D

Levels: 1

Heated Square Footage: 1,891

Bedrooms: 3

Bathrooms: 2

Foundation: Crawl space; slab or basement for fee

Materials List Available: No

Price Category: E

If you prefer the look of Craftsman homes, you'll love the details this plan includes. Wide-based columns across the front porch, Mission-style windows, and a balanced mixture of exterior materials add up to true good looks.

Features:

• Great Room: A built-in media center and a fireplace in this room make it distinctive.

• Kitchen: A huge skylight over an island eating counter brightens this kitchen. A private office space opens through double doors nearby.

• Dining Room: This room has sliding glass doors opening to the rear patio.

• Bedrooms: Two bedrooms with two bathrooms are located on the right side of the plan. One of the bedrooms is the master suite with a vaulted bath with a spa tub.

• Garage: You'll be able to reach this two-car garage via a service hallway that contains a laundry room, a walk-in pantry, and a closet.

Images provided by designer/architect.

Copyright by designer/architect.

Rear Elevation

Images provided by designer/architect.

Plan #F01-131011

Dimensions: 75'2" W x 60'9" D
Levels: 1
Heated Square Footage: 1,897
Bedrooms: 4
Bathrooms: 2
Foundation: Crawl space or slab;
basement for fee
Materials List Available: Yes
Price Category: E

You'll love this home if you're looking for a plan for a sloping lot or flat one or if you want to orient the rear porch to face into or away from the sun.

Features:

- Ceiling Height: 8 ft.

- Living Area: The whole family will find it easy to congregate in this lovely room.

- Kitchen: The angle of the home makes the kitchen especially convenient, while also giving it an unusual amount of character.

- Study: Located near the front door, this room can serve as a home office or fourth bedroom as easily as it does a private study.

- Master Suite: Located at the opposite end of the home from the other two bedrooms, this master suite offers privacy and quiet.

- Additional Bedrooms: These two bedrooms share a distinctive hall bathroom.

Rear View

Plan #F01-131016

Dimensions: 75' W x 45' D

Levels: 1

Heated Square Footage: 1,902

Bedrooms: 3

Bathrooms: 2

Foundation: Crawl space or slab, basement for fee

Materials List Available: Yes

Price Category: E

Images provided by designer/architect.

If traditional country looks appeal to you, you'll be delighted by the wraparound covered porch that forms the entryway to this comfortable home.

Features:

- **Great Room:** Sit by the fireplace in this room with feature walls so large that they'll suit a home theater or large media center.

- **Kitchen:** Overlooking the great room, this well-designed kitchen has great cabinets and ample counter space to make all your cooking and cleaning a pleasure.

- **Master Suite:** A large bay window makes the bedroom in this private suite sophisticated, and two walk-in closets make it practical. You'll love to relax in the master bath, whether in the whirlpool tub or the separate shower. A dual-sink vanity completes the amenities in this room.

- **Garage:** Find extra storage space in this two-bayed, attached garage.

Copyright by designer/architect.

Great Room

Images provided by designer/architect.

Plan #F01-121001

Dimensions: 56' W x 58' D

Levels: 1

Heated Square Footage: 1,911

Bedrooms: 3

Bathrooms: 2

Foundation: Basement

Materials List Available: Yes

Price Category: D

Detailed, soaring ceilings and top-notch amenities set this distinctive home apart.

Features:

- Ceiling Height: 8 ft. except as noted.

- Formal Dining Room: The entry enjoys a pleasing view of this dining room's detailed 12-ft. ceiling and picture window.

- Great Room: At the back of the home, a see-through fireplace in this great room is joined by a built-in entertainment center.

- Hearth Room: This bayed room shares the see-through fireplace with the great room.

- Master Suite: Enjoy the stars and the sun in the private master bath's whirlpool thanks to the skylight above. The bath features the same decorative ceiling as the dining room.

Storage Options for Your Home

One of the great things about moving into a new home is all that new, uncluttered closet space you gain. But if you are like most homeowners, storage of all types will quickly become scarce, especially in a smaller home. Here are some tips for expanding and organizing storage space.

Shelving Types

Shelving is an easy and economical way to add extra storage space in almost any part of your home — along walls, inside closets, and even in the basement or garage. Building shelves doesn't usually require a lot of skill or specialized tools, so this is one project just about any do-it-yourselfer can handle. And unless you decide to use hardwood — which looks great, but costs a bundle — it won't cost a lot to install them either.

Solid wood shelving is the way to go when you want to show off the wood or your work.

Plywood and particleboard offer a couple of advantages when it comes to shelving, though. They cost less than solid wood, and can be bought faced with decorative surfaces. They also come in sheets, which makes them ideal for a really wide shelf. Inexpensive, manufactured storage units

Home offices require a mix of storage options: open shelving, drawers, and file cabinets.

ready for assembly often are made from melamine-coated particleboard.

Wood trim will help match your new shelves to the rest of the room or add some interesting detail. Trim is also a handy way to hide seams, gaps, exposed edges of plywood, and other blemishes. You can get trim in either hardwood or softwood. If you plan on finishing a project with stain or sealer, make sure the trim matches the wood you used for the rest of the project.

Bracket Options

There are two basic types of ready-to-hang shelving supports: stationary shelf brackets and shelving standards. Stationary brackets come in many sizes and styles, and range from utilitarian to decorative. Shelving standards are slotted metal strips that support various types of shelf brackets.

Mounting Brackets

For maximum strength, anchor shelf supports to wall studs. If your shelf will carry a light load, you can anchor its supports between studs with mollies or toggle bolts. Attaching supports directly to the studs is always better, though, because sooner or later something heavy will wind up on the shelf. Use masonry anchors to attach shelf supports to brick or concrete. You can also attach shelf supports to a ledger attached to wall studs with 3-inch drywall screws.

Ready-made shelving offers a quick alternative to building your own shelves.

Mud rooms and areas near the entrance the family uses most should have storage for coats, hats, and boots.

Shelf Standards. Metal shelf standards can be mounted directly to walls or, for a more decorative look, you can insert the standards in grooves routed into the wood itself or into hardwood strips.

Cut the standards to fit with a hacksaw, and attach them to wall studs with 3-inch drywall screws. Use a carpenter's level to make sure that both standards are plumb and that the corresponding mounting slots are level. Mount standards 6 inches from the ends of shelving to prevent sagging. For long wall shelves, install standards every 48 inches.

Many kitchen and closet storage systems use wire grids that attach to walls with molded plastic brackets. If you anticipate light loads, you can mount these brackets to drywall using the screws and expansion anchors usually included with such systems. But for heavier loads, use drywall screws to fasten the brackets directly to the wall studs.

Customized Storage

Built-in storage units are an excellent way to make the most of existing storage space in your home. Ready-made or custom-made built-in shelving units, entertainment centers, kitchen cabinets, medicine cabinets, window seats, and under-bed drawers are not only inexpensive and easy to assemble, they allow you to add a unique, personalized touch to your living spaces.

Built-in Shelving

A built-in shelving unit can create valuable storage capacity from an overlooked wall space, such as the area between windows or between a door and its adjacent corner. To construct the shelving, you'll need 1×10 or 1×12 lumber for side panels, top and base panels, and shelves; four 2×2 strips for spreaders; trim molding to conceal gaps along the top and bottom of the unit; 12d common nails and 6d finishing nails.

If the unit will be bearing heavy loads, use hardwood boards, and make sure that the shelves span no more than 36 inches. To make installation easier, cut the side pieces an inch shorter than the ceiling height. (This way, you'll be able to tilt the unit into position without scraping the ceiling.) Paint or stain the wood pieces before assembling the unit. Hang the shelves from pegs or end clips inserted into holes drilled in the side pieces.

Adding Closet Space

What homeowner, even a new homeowner, hasn't complained about having too little closet space? Fortunately, there are almost always ways to find a bit more closet space or to make the closet space you have more efficient. Often, it isn't the space that is lacking but how the space is organized that is the problem. The trick is to find ways to help you organize the space.

Ventilated closet systems help keep your belongings neat and within easy reach.

Organizing Systems. The easiest and most obvious solution is one of the many commercial closet organizing systems now on the market. There are a number of configurations available, and you can customize most systems to meet your needs. Constructing your own version of a commercial closet organizer is another option. With a combination of shelves and plywood partitions, you can divide a closet into storage zones, with a single clothes pole on one side for full-length garments; double clothes poles on the other side for half-length garments like jackets, skirts, or slacks; a column of narrow shelves between the two for folded items or shoes; and one or more closet-wide shelves on top.

Before designing a closet system, above, inventory all of the items you want to store in the closet.

Metal shelf standards, left, can provide a quick solution for creating shelving in areas where it is needed.

Cedar Closets

Both solid cedar boards and composite cedar panels have only moderate resistance to insects, and are used more for their pleasant aroma and appearance. The sheets of pressed red and tan particles are no less aromatic than solid wood, but the panels are 40 to 50 percent less expensive, and are easier to install. Solid boards require more carpentry work, and are likely to produce a fair amount of waste unless you piece the courses and create more joints. To gain the maximum effect, every inside surface should be covered, including the ceiling and the back of the door. The simplest option is to use ¼-inch-thick panels, which are easy to cut into big sections that cover walls in one or two pieces. Try to keep cedar seams in boards or panels from falling over drywall seams. No stain, sealer, or clear finish is needed; just leave the wood raw. The cedar aroma will fade over the years as natural oils crystallize on

For garages and basements, you'll find a combination of shelving and hanging hooks keeps tools and equipment organized, opposite top.

Storage for basements, garages, and workshops, opposite bottom, should include a cabinet that locks for storage of dangerous chemicals.

Specialized storage accessories, such as the sports storage system shown at right, not only keeps items organized but they also keep them in ready-to-play condition.

the surface. But you can easily regenerate the scent from the panels by scuffing the surface with fine sandpaper.

Ideas for Basements, Garages, and Workshops

Workshops and other utility areas such as garages, attics, and basements can benefit from storage upgrades as much as any other room in the home — perhaps even more so, as utility areas are prone to clutter. Convenience, flexibility, and safety are the things to keep in mind when reorganizing your work space. Try to provide storage space for tools and hardware as near as possible to where they'll be used. In addition to a sturdy

workbench, utility shelving is a mainstay in any workshop. You can buy ready-to-assemble units or make your own using ¾-inch particleboard or plywood shelves and ¾ × 1½-inch (1×2) hardwood stock for cleats (nailed to the wall), ribs (nailed to the front underside of the shelves), and vertical shelf supports.

DIY Utility Storage. Don't forget about pegboard. To make a pegboard tool rack, attach washers to the back of the pegboard with hot glue, spacing the washers to coincide with wall studs. Position the pegboard so that the rear washers are located over studs. Drive drywall screws through finish washers and the pegboard into studs. (Use masonry anchors for concrete walls.)

Finally, try to take advantage of any otherwise wasted space. The area in your garage above your parked car is the ideal spot for a U-shaped lumber storage rack, made of 1×4 stock and connecting plates. The space in front of the car could be used for a storage cabinet or even a workbench.

Instant Storage. To utilize the overhead space in your garage, build deep storage platforms supported by ledgers screwed to wall studs and threaded rods hooked to ceiling joists or rafters. You can also hang tools from the walls by mounting pegboard. You can buy sets with a variety of hooks and brackets for tools. For small items, such as jars of nails, make shallow shelves by nailing 1×4 boards between the exposed studs.

Kitchen Storage

The type of storage in a kitchen is almost as important as the amount. Some people like at least a few open shelves for displaying attractive china or glassware; others want absolutely everything tucked away behind doors.

What are your storage needs? The answer depends partly on your food shopping habits and partly on how many pots, pans, and other pieces of kitchen equipment you have or would like to have. A family that goes food shopping several times a week and prepares mostly fresh foods needs more refrigerator space, less freezer capacity, and fewer cabinets than a family that prefers packaged or prepared foods and makes only infrequent forays to the local supermarket.

Planning

To help clarify your needs, mentally walk yourself through a typical meal and list the utensils used to prepare food, where you got them, and your progress throughout the work area. And don't limit yourself to full-scale meals. Much kitchen work is devoted to preparing snacks, reheating leftovers, and making lunches for the kids to take to school.

Food Preparation. During food preparation, the sink and stove come into use. Some families rely heavily on the microwave for reheating. Using water means repeated trips to the sink, so that area might be the best place to keep a steamer, salad spinner, and coffee and tea canisters, as well as glassware and cups. Near the stove you may want storage for odd-shaped items such as a fish poacher or wok. You can hang frequently used pans and utensils from a convenient rack; stow other items in cabinets so that they do not collect grease.

During the Meal. When the food is ready, you must take it to the table. If the eating space is nearby, a work counter might turn into a serving counter. If the dining space is in another room, a pass-through facilitates serving.

Storage accessories, such as the pullout pot holder above, come as options from some cabinet manufacturers, or you can install them later yourself. Notice how the side rails hold the pot lids in place. The cabinet below features space for small baskets.

After the Meal. When the meal ends, dishes must go from the table to the sink or dishwasher, and leftovers to storage containers and the refrigerator. Now the stove and counters need to be wiped down and the sink scoured. When the dishwasher finishes its cycle, everything must be put away.

Open versus Closed Storage. Shelves, pegboards, pot racks, cup hooks, magnetic knife racks, and the like put your utensils on view, which is a good way to personalize your kitchen.

But open storage has drawbacks. Items left out in the open can look messy unless they are kept neatly arranged. Another option is to install glass doors on wall cabinets. This handily solves the dust problem but often costs more than solid doors.

Plan #F01-151089

Dimensions: 84" W x 55'6" D
Levels: 1
Heated Square Footage: 1,921
Bedrooms: 3
Bathrooms: 3
Foundation: Crawl space or slab; basement or walkout for fee
Materials List Available: No
Price Category: I

If your family loves to combine indoor and outdoor living, this home's fabulous porches and deck space make it perfect.

Features:

- Porches: A huge wraparound front porch, sizable rear porch, and deck that joins them give you space for entertaining or simply lounging.

- Living Room: A fireplace and built-in media center could be the focal points in this large room.

- Hearth Room: Open to both the living room and kitchen, this hearth room also features a fireplace.

- Kitchen: This step-saving kitchen includes ample storage and work space, as well as an angled bar it shares with the hearth room. Atrium doors lead to the rear porch.

- Bonus Upper Level: A large game room and a full bath make this area a favorite with the children.

Images provided by designer/architect.

Bonus Area

Copyright by designer/architect.

Images provided by designer/architect.

Plan #F01-221015

Dimensions: 69'8" W x 46' D

Levels: 1

Heated Square Footage: 1,926

Bedrooms: 3

Bathrooms: 2½

Foundation: Basement; crawl space, slab or walkout basement for fee

Materials List Available: No

Price Category: D

CAD FILE AVAILABLE

You'll love the open plan in this lovely ranch and admire its many features, which are usually reserved for much larger homes.

Features:

- Ceiling Height: 8 ft.

- Great Room: A vaulted ceiling and tall windows surrounding the centrally located fireplace give distinction to this handsome room.

- Dining Room: Positioned just off the entry, this formal room makes a lovely spot for quiet dinner parties.

- Dining Nook: This nook sits between the kitchen and the great room. Central doors in the bayed area open to the backyard.

- Kitchen: An island will invite visitors while you cook in this well-planned kitchen, with its corner pantry and ample counter space.

- Master Suite: A tray ceiling, bay window, walk-in closet, and bath with whirlpool tub, dual-sink vanity, and standing shower pamper you here.

Rear Elevation

Copyright by designer/architect.

Plan #F01-301005

Dimensions: 71' W x 42' D
Levels: 1
Heated Square Footage: 1,930
Bedrooms: 3
Bathrooms: 2
Foundation: Crawl space or slab
Materials List Available: Yes
Price Category: D

This home features an old-fashioned rocking-chair porch that enhances the streetscape.

Features:

• Ceiling Height: 8 ft.

• Dining Room: When the weather is warm, guests can step through French doors from this elegant dining room and enjoy a breeze on the rear screened porch.

• Family Room: This family room is a warm and inviting place to gather, with its handsome fireplace and built-in bookcases.

• Kitchen: This kitchen offers plenty of counter space for preparing your favorite recipes. Its U-shape creates a convenient open traffic pattern.

• Master Suite: You'll look forward to retiring at the end of the day in this truly luxurious master suite. The bedroom has a fireplace and opens through French doors to a private rear deck. The bath features a corner spa tub, a walk-in shower, a double-bowl vanity, and a linen closet.

Images provided by designer/architect.

Copyright by designer/architect.

SMARTtip

Light With Shutters

For the maximum amount of light coming through shutters, use the largest panel possible on the window. Make sure the shutters have the same number of louvers per panel so that all of the windows in the room look unified. However, don't choose a panel that is over 48 inches high, because the shutter becomes unwieldy. Also, any window that is wider than 96 inches requires extra framing to support the shutters.

Plan #F01-271073

Dimensions: 69' W x 56' D
Levels: 1
Heated Square Footage: 1,920
Bedrooms: 3
Bathrooms: 2½
Foundation: Walkout basement
Materials List Available: No
Price Category: D

Images provided by designer/architect.

A great floor plan and plenty of space make this home perfect for people who welcome family members back home to visit.

Features:

• Great Room: This vaulted space shares a see-through fireplace with a cozy hearth room.

• Kitchen: An angled island and a step-in pantry are the highlights of this room.

• Study: Double doors introduce this versatile space, which shows off a nice bay window.

• Master Suite: Double doors lead to the bedroom. The private bath hosts a whirlpool tub and a separate shower.

• Basement: This level contains more bedrooms and family spaces for visiting relatives.

Basement Level

Copyright by designer/architect.

Plan #F01-481154

Dimensions: 77' W x 65' D

Levels: 1

Heated Square Footage: 1,918

Bedrooms: 2

Bathrooms: 1½

Foundation: Walkout basement

Material List Available: No

Price Category: D

Images provided by designer/architect.

CAD FILE AVAILABLE CAD

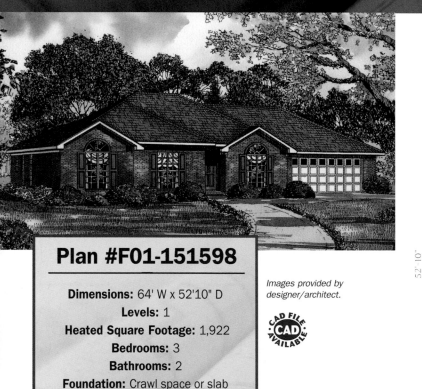

Plan #F01-151598

Dimensions: 64' W x 52'10" D

Levels: 1

Heated Square Footage: 1,922

Bedrooms: 3

Bathrooms: 2

Foundation: Crawl space or slab

Materials List Available: No

Price Category: H

Images provided by designer/architect.

CAD FILE AVAILABLE CAD

Plan #F01-351186

Dimensions: 68' W x 59'10" D

Levels: 1

Heated Square Footage: 1,924

Bedrooms: 3

Bathrooms: 2

Foundation: Basement

Materials List Available: Yes

Price Category: H

Images provided by designer/architect.

CAD FILE AVAILABLE

Plan #F01-351205

Dimensions: 70'8" W x 60' D

Levels: 1

Heated Square Footage: 1,934

Bedrooms: 3

Bathrooms: 2

Foundation: Crawl space or slab

Materials List Available: Yes

Price Category: H

Images provided by designer/architect.

CAD FILE AVAILABLE

Rear Elevation

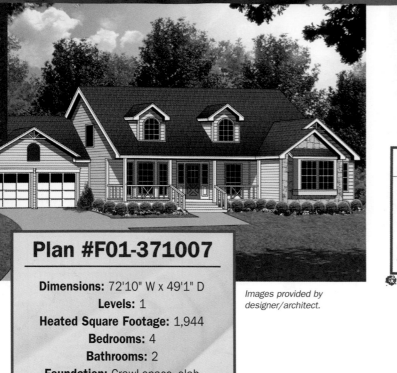

Plan #F01-371007

Dimensions: 72'10" W x 49'1" D

Levels: 1

Heated Square Footage: 1,944

Bedrooms: 4

Bathrooms: 2

Foundation: Crawl space, slab or basement

Materials List Available: No

Price Category: D

Images provided by designer/architect.

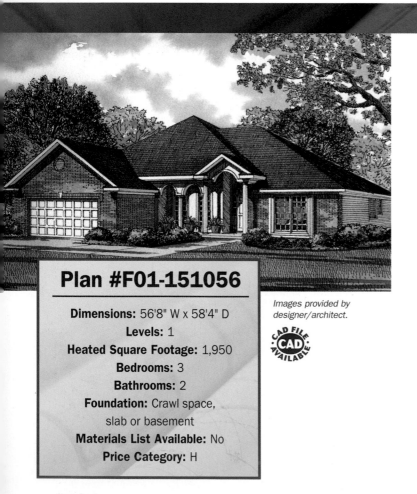

Plan #F01-151056

Dimensions: 56'8" W x 58'4" D

Levels: 1

Heated Square Footage: 1,950

Bedrooms: 3

Bathrooms: 2

Foundation: Crawl space, slab or basement

Materials List Available: No

Price Category: H

Images provided by designer/architect.

CAD FILE AVAILABLE

Plan #F01-761039

Dimensions: 61' W x 40'4" D

Levels: 1

Heated Square Footage: 1,624

Bedrooms: 3

Bathrooms: 2

Foundation: Basement

Materials List Available: Yes

Price Category: C

Images provided by designer/architect.

Copyright by designer/architect.

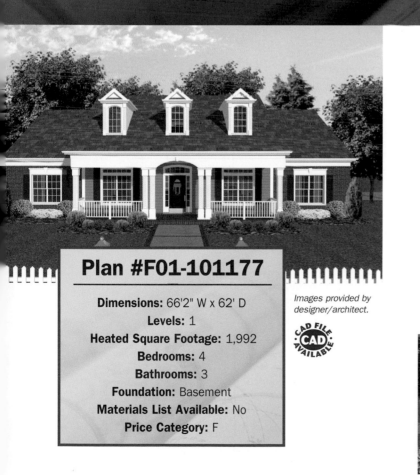

Plan #F01-101177

Dimensions: 66'2" W x 62' D

Levels: 1

Heated Square Footage: 1,992

Bedrooms: 4

Bathrooms: 3

Foundation: Basement

Materials List Available: No

Price Category: F

Images provided by designer/architect.

Copyright by designer/architect.

Rear View

Images provided by designer/architect.

Plan #F01-151117

Dimensions: 66' W x 55' D
Levels: 1
Heated Square Footage: 1,957
Bedrooms: 3
Bathrooms: 3
Foundation: Crawl space or slab; walkout or basement for fee
Materials List Available: No
Price Category: H

You'll love this home if you have a family - centered lifestyle and enjoy an active social life.

Features:

- Foyer: A 10-ft. ceiling sets the tone for this home.

- Great Room: A 10-ft. boxed ceiling and fireplace are the highlights of this room, which also has a door leading to the rear covered porch.

- Dining Room: Columns mark the entry from the foyer to this lovely formal dining room.

- Study: Add the French doors from the foyer to transform bedroom 3, with its vaulted ceiling, into a quiet study.

- Kitchen: This large kitchen includes a pantry and shares an eating bar with the adjoining, bayed breakfast room.

- Master Suite: You'll love the access to the rear porch, as well as the bath with every amenity, in this suite.

Bonus Area

Copyright by designer/architect.

Images provided by designer/architect.

Plan #F01-101028

Dimensions: 57'8" W x 57'6" D

Levels: 1

Heated Square Footage: 1,963

Bedrooms: 3

Bathrooms: 2

Foundation: Basement;
crawl space or slab for fee

Materials List Available: No

Price Category: F

This elegant brick-and-stone home is a real eye-catcher.

Features:

- Dining Room: Just off the foyer, this formal area is open to the family room.

- Family Room: This large gathering area has a cozy fireplace and flows into the screened in porch.

- Kitchen: This U-shaped "heart of the home" is open to the breakfast area.

- Master Suite: This private retreat has everything; a tray ceiling, a sitting area, and a large bathroom with a double-bowl vanity.

- Bedrooms: Located on the opposite side of the home from the master suite, the two secondary bedrooms have walk-in closets and share a bathroom.

CAD FILE AVAILABLE

BONUS ROOM
14'-2" x 30'-2"
309 Sq. Ft.

Bonus Area

SITTING

MASTER SUITE
23'-4" x 15'
Tray Ceiling

DECK
17'-4" x 12'

BEDROOM 3
13' x 12'-10"

SCREENED PORCH
17'-4" x 7'-10"
Skylight   Skylight

KITCHEN
12'-9" x 10'

DW

Pantry

BREAKFAST
12'-3" x 12'-2"

KS

Coats   Desk

Stairs to Bonus Room

Stairs to Base-ment

FAMILY
18' x 16'-2"

Lin

BEDROOM 2
13' x 11'

2-CAR SIDE-LOAD GARAGE
23'-4" x 20'-2"

DINING
11' x 15'-4"

PORCH
19'-8" x 7'-4"

57'-6"

57'-8"

Copyright by designer/architect.

Plan #F01-151170

Dimensions: 57' W x 64'4" D
Levels: 1
Heated Square Footage: 1,965
Bedrooms: 4
Bathrooms: 2
Foundation: Crawl space or slab; basement or walkout basement for fee
Materials List Available: No
Price Category: I

The clean lines of the open floor plan and high ceilings match the classic good looks of this home's exterior.

Features:

- Foyer: The 10-ft. ceiling here sets the stage for the open, airy feeling of this lovely home.

- Dining Room: Set off by columns from the foyer and great room, this area is ideal for entertaining.

- Great Room: Open to the breakfast room beyond, this great room features a masonry fireplace and a door to the rear grilling porch.

- Breakfast Room: A deep bay overlooking the porch is the focal point here.

- Kitchen: Planned for efficiency, the kitchen has an angled island with storage and snack bar.

- Master Suite: A boxed ceiling adds elegance to the bedroom, and the bath features a whirlpool tub, double vanity, and separate shower.

Images provided by designer/architect.

Copyright by designer/architect.

Bonus Area

Images provided by designer/architect.

Plan #F01-761004

Dimensions: 68'4" W x 56' D

Levels: 1

Heated Square Footage: 2,241

Bedrooms: 4

Bathrooms: 2½

Foundation: Basement

Materials List Available: Yes

Price Category: E

This home's see-through, freestanding fireplace is the center of attention from all angles inside the home.

Features:

- Great Room, Kitchen and Dining Areas: 11' ceilings can be found in the entry, great room, kitchen and the dining area.

- Kitchen: The large kitchen island breakfast bar also includes a table extension providing enough dining space for up to seven people.

- Master Suite: The elegant master bedroom is topped with a coffered ceiling and enjoys amenities such as two walk-in closets and a private bath.

- Energy-Efficient Walls: This home has the option of 2x6 exterior walls instead of 2x4. The extra thickness makes room for more insulation to lower your heating and cooling bills.

Kitchen Views

Images provided by designer/architect.

Plan #F01-101006

Dimensions: 63' W x 58' D
Levels: 1
Heated Square Footage: 1,982
Bedrooms: 3
Bathrooms: 2½
Foundation: Walkout, basement, slab or crawl space
Materials List Available: Yes
Price Category: F

Radius-top windows and siding accented with wood shingles give this home a distinctive look.

Features:

• **Ceiling Height:** 9 ft. unless otherwise noted.

• **Family Room:** This room is perfect for all kinds of informal family activities. A vaulted ceiling adds to its sense of spaciousness.

• **Dining Room:** This room, with its tray ceiling, is designed for elegant dining.

• **Porch:** When the weather gets warm, you'll enjoy stepping out onto this large screened porch to catch a breeze.

• **Master Suite:** You'll love ending your day and getting up in the morning in this exquisite master suite, with its vaulted ceiling, sitting area, and large walk-in closet.

• **Bonus Room:** Just off the kitchen are stairs leading to this enormous bonus room, offering more than 330 sq. ft. of future expansion space.

Copyright by designer/architect.

SMARTtip

Art in Pools

The tiled walls and floor of a pool make great canvases for art, so incorporate a serious or whimsical design. Also, make the stairs wide and shallow to form a wading area for kids.

Images provided by designer/architect.

Plan #F01-181159

Dimensions: 37' W x 31' D

Levels: 1

Heated Square Footage: 1,992

Main Level Sq. Ft.: 996

Lower Level Sq. Ft.: 996

Bedrooms: 3

Bathrooms: 2

Foundation: Walkout basement

Materials List Available: Yes

Price Category: G

Ideal for the family who loves the outdoors, this charmer features a wraparound porch that creates a covered pavilion and roofed terrace.

Features:

- Ceiling Height: 9-ft. ceilings enhance the airy feeling given by the many windows here.

- Family Rooms: These family rooms (one on each floor) allow a busy family adequate space for entertaining a crowd.

- Kitchen: Designed for efficient work patterns, this kitchen features ample work and storage space, as well as an island that can double as an eating bar

- Bedrooms: Each bedroom features a large, walk-in closet and easy access to a large, amenity-filled bathroom with a double-bowl vanity, tub, enclosed shower, and private toilet.

- Porch: Enjoy the panoramic view from this spacious covered porch at any time of day.

Copyright by designer/architect.

CAD FILE AVAILABLE

31'-0"
9,3 m

37'-0"
11,1 m

19'-8" X 11'-0"
5,90 X 3,30

10'-0" X 12'-0"
3,00 X 3,60

8'-0" X 13'-0"
2,40 X 3,90

10'-0" X 16'-0"
3,00 X 4,80

Main Level

19'-4" X 15'-0"
5,80 X 4,50

10'-0" X 15'-0"
3,00 X 4,50

10'-0" X 15'-8"
3,00 X 4,70

Lower Level

Plan #F01-101005

Dimensions: 63' W x 57'2" D

Levels: 1

Heated Square Footage: 1,992

Bedrooms: 3

Bathrooms: 2½

Foundation: Crawl space, slab, or basement

Materials List Available: Yes

Price Category: F

Images provided by designer/architect.

Rear View

This midsized ranch is accented with Palladian windows and an inviting front porch.

Features:

- Ceiling Height: 9 ft. unless otherwise noted.

- Special Ceilings: Tray or vaulted ceilings adorn the living room, family room, dining room, and master suite.

- Kitchen: This bright and airy kitchen is designed to be a pleasure in which to work. It shares a big bay window with the contiguous breakfast room.

- Breakfast Room: The light streaming in from the bay window makes this the perfect place to linger with coffee and the Sunday paper.

- Master Suite: This lovely suite is exceptional, with its sitting area and direct access to the deck, as well as a full-featured bath and spacious walk-in closet.

- Secondary Bedrooms: The other bedrooms each measure about 13 ft. x 11 ft. They have walk-in closets and share a "Jack-and-Jill" bath.

Copyright by designer/architect.

Kitchen

Living Room

Dining Room

Family Room

Master Bedroom

Master Bath

Plan #F01-131044

Dimensions: 57'6" W x 42'4" D
Levels: 1
Heated Square Footage: 1,994
Bedrooms: 4
Bathrooms: 2
Foundation: Crawl space or slab;
basement for fee
Materials List Available: Yes
Price Category: E

Under a covered porch, Victorian-detailed bay windows grace each side of the brick-faced facade at the center of this ranch-style home, giving it a formal air.

Images provided by designer/architect.

Features:

- **Ceiling Height:** 10-ft. ceilings grace the central living area and the master bedroom of this home.

- **Foyer:** Round-top windows make this area and the flanking rooms bright and cheery.

- **Great Room:** A fireplace and built-ins that are visible from anywhere in this large room make it a natural gathering place for friends and family.

- **Optional Office:** Use the room just off the central hall as a home office, fourth bedroom, or study.

- **Master Suite:** You'll love the bay window, tray ceiling, two walk-in closets, and private bath.

- **Bonus Space:** Finish this large area in the attic for extra living space, or use it for storage.

Rear Elevation

Bonus Area

Plan #F01-121050

Dimensions: 64' W x 50' D
Levels: 1
Heated Square Footage: 1,996
Bedrooms: 2
Bathrooms: 2
Foundation: Basement; crawl space for fee
Materials List Available: Yes
Price Category: D

Images provided by designer/architect.

This compact design includes features usually reserved for larger homes and has styling that is typical of luxury home designs.

Features:

- **Entry:** As you enter this home, you'll see the formal living and dining rooms — both with special ceiling detailing — on either side.

- **Great Room:** Located in the rear of the home for convenience, this great room is likely to be your favorite spot. The fireplace is framed by transom-topped windows, so you'll love curling up here, no matter what the weather, or time of day.

- **Kitchen:** Ample counter and cabinet space make this kitchen a dream in which to work.

- **Master Suite:** A tray ceiling and lovely corner windows create an elegant feeling in the bedroom, and two walk-in closets make it easy to keep this space tidy and organized. The private bath has a skylight, corner whirlpool tub, and two separate vanities.

Images provided by designer/architect.

Plan #F01-371042

Dimensions: 71'6" W x 49' D
Levels: 1
Heated Square Footage: 1,999
Bedrooms: 3
Bathrooms: 2
Foundation: Crawl space, slab or basement
Materials List Available: No
Price Category: D

Ornate windows accent the exterior of this elegant French-style home — a dream come true.

Features:

- **Entry:** The raised porch will lead you into this beautiful tiled entry, with a barrel ceiling and columns separating it from a formal dining room.

- **Living Room:** This massive room has a double stepped-up ceiling and access to the rear porch. There is a built-in media center and charming fireplace.

- **Kitchen:** This gourmet kitchen with breakfast nook has a serving bar, which opens into the living room.

- **Master Suite:** This suite also has a stepped-up ceiling and a luxurious master bath with a double-bowl vanity and two walk-in closets.

- **Bedrooms:** Two additional large bedrooms share a convenient hall bathroom.

Plan #F01-211005

Dimensions: 68' W x 64' D
Levels: 1
Heated Square Footage: 2,000
Bedrooms: 3
Bathrooms: 2
Foundation: Slab; crawl space for fee
Materials List Available: Yes
Price Category: D

A brick veneer exterior complements the columned porch to make this a striking home.

Images provided by designer/architect.

Features:

- Ceiling Height: 9 ft. unless otherwise noted.

- Living Room: From the front porch, the foyer unfolds into this expansive living room. Family and friends will be drawn to the warmth of the living room's cozy fireplace.

- Formal Dining Room: This elegant room is designed for dinner parties of any size.

- Kitchen: Located between the formal dining room and the breakfast room, the kitchen can serve formal meals as easily as casual.

- Master Suite: There's plenty of room to unwind at the end of a long day in the huge master bedroom. Relax in the private bath, with its spa tub, separate shower, dual sinks, and two walk-in closets.

- Home Office: The home office, accessible from the master bedroom, is the perfect quiet spot to work, study, or pay the bills.

SMARTtip

Do-It-Yourself Ponds

To avoid disturbing utility lines, contact your utility companies before doing any digging. Locate a freestanding container pond on your deck near an existing (GFCI) outlet. For an in-ground pond, have an electrician run a buried line and install a GFCI outlet near the pond so you can plug in a pump or fountain.

Copyright by designer/architect.

Plan #F01-101022

Dimensions: 66'2" W x 62' D
Levels: 1
Heated Square Footage: 1,992
Bedrooms: 3
Bathrooms: 3
Foundation: Crawl space, slab, or basement
Materials List Available: Yes
Price Category: F

Images provided by designer/architect.

The exterior of this lovely home is traditional, but the unusually shaped rooms and amenities are contemporary.

Features:

- Foyer: This two-story foyer is open to the family room, but columns divide it from the dining room.

- Family Room: A gas fireplace and TV niche, flanked by doors to the covered porch, sit at the rear of this seven-sided, spacious room.

- Breakfast Room: Set off from the family room by columns, this area shares a snack bar with the kitchen and has windows looking over the porch.

- Bedroom 3: Use this room as a living room if you wish, and transform the guest room to a media room or a family bedroom.

- Master Suite: The bedroom features a tray ceiling, has his and her dressing areas, and opens to the porch. The bath has a large corner tub, separate shower, linen closet, and two vanities.

Copyright by designer/architect.

Kitchen

Great Room

Dining Room

Hearth Room

Master Bedroom

Study

Plan #F01-351047

Dimensions: 64' W x 54'4" D

Levels: 1

Heated Square Footage: 2,001

Bedrooms: 3

Bathrooms: 2

Foundation: Crawl space, slab, or basement

Materials List Available: Yes

Price Category: H

Images provided by designer/architect.

This home incorporates a unique design that maximizes every inch of its usable space to give you more for less.

Features:

• Great Room: This large room features a vaulted ceiling and a gas fireplace that has built-in cabinets on each side.

• Kitchen: This kitchen has a raised bar and is open to the sunroom and dining room.

• Dining Room: This gracious room has a view of the backyard and a raised ceiling.

• Master Suite: This area boasts a raised ceiling and a walk-in closet. There is also a private master bath with another walk-in closet.

• Bedrooms: These two additional bedrooms share a bathroom located in the hall.

Copyright by designer/architect.

Images provided by designer/architect.

Plan #F01-151138

Dimensions: 53' W x 49'4" D
Levels: 1
Heated Square Footage: 2,010
Bedrooms: 3
Bathrooms: 2
Foundation: Basement or walkout
Materials List Available: No
Price Category: H

This versatile offering fits anywhere. Its design is as comfortable in the city as it is in the country.

Features:

- Porches: Two porches—a covered porch at the front of the home and a grilling porch at the back—are wonderful for entertaining or relaxing.
- Great Room: This beautiful great room is a wonderful, versatile space, with its vaulted ceiling and fireplace.
- Kitchen: In this kitchen, there is space for cooks and diners alike, thanks to the spacious countertop and raised eating bar. For a more formal setting, there is an adjoining dining room.
- Master Suite: Spacious areas define this wonderful master suite, with its large bedroom area and sizable walk-in closet.

Main Level

Lower Level

Copyright by designer/architect.

Images provided by designer/architect.

Plan #F01-211049

Dimensions: 73' W x 66' D
Levels: 1
Heated Square Footage: 2,023
Bedrooms: 3
Bathrooms: 2
Foundation: Slab; crawl space for fee
Materials List Available: Yes
Price Category: D

CAD FILE AVAILABLE

This European-style home features an open floor plan that maximizes use and flexibility of space.

Features:

- Ceiling Height: 8 ft. unless otherwise noted.

- Living/Dining Area: This combined living - and-dining area features high ceilings, which make the large area seem even more spacious. Corner windows fill the room with light. The wet bar and cozy fireplace make this the perfect place for entertaining.

- Backyard Covered Porch: This huge covered backyard porch is accessible from the living/

dining area, so the entire party can step outdoors on a warm summer night.

- Kitchen: More than just efficient, this modern kitchen is actually an exciting place to cook. It features a dramatic high ceiling and plenty of work space.

- Utility Area: Located off the kitchen, this area has extra freezer space, a walk-in pantry, and access to the garage.

- Eating Nook: Informal family meals will be a true delight in this nook that adjoins the kitchen and faces a lovely private courtyard.

Copyright by designer/architect.

garage 22 x 22

sto

sto

porch

util

pan

courtyard

eating 11 x 10

dining 12 x 12
12' clg.

kit

living 22 x 21
12' clg.

books

br 3 12 x 12

clo

lin

mbr 20 x 14

porch

wet bar

br 2 13 x 13

books

clo

SMARTtip

Outdoor Lighting Safety

Lighting is necessary for walkways, paths, stairways, and transition areas (from the deck to the yard, hot tub, or pool) to prevent accidents. Choose from low-voltage rail, path, and post lighting for these areas. The corners of planters or built-in seating should also be delineated with lighting. Consider installing floodlights near doorways or large open spaces for security reasons.

Images provided by designer/architect.

Plan #F01-351008

Dimensions: 64'6" W x 61'4" D

Levels: 1

Heated Square Footage: 2,002

Bedrooms: 3

Bathrooms: 2

Foundation: Basement, crawl space or slab

Materials List Available: Yes

Price Category: H

This home has the charming appeal of a quaint cottage that you might find in an old village in the English countryside. It's a unique design that maximizes every inch of its usable space.

Features:

- Great Room: This room has a vaulted ceiling and built-in units on each side of the fireplace.

- Kitchen: This kitchen boasts a raised bar open to the breakfast area; the room is also open to the dining room.

- Master Suite: This bedroom retreat features a raised ceiling and a walk-in closet. The bathroom has a double vanity, large walk-in closet, and soaking tub.

- Bedrooms: Two bedrooms share a common bathroom and have large closets.

Copyright by designer/architect.

Plan #F01-761049

Dimensions: 56'8" W x 59' D

Levels: 2

Heated Square Footage: 2,100

Bedrooms: 3

Bathrooms: 2

Foundation: Basement

Materials List Available: Yes

Price Category: C

Images provided by designer/architect.

CAD FILE AVAILABLE

Main Level

Basement Level

Plan #F01-101169

Dimensions: 63' W x 62'8" D

Levels: 1

Heated Square Footage: 2,000

Bedrooms: 3

Bathrooms: 2½

Foundation: Basement

Materials List Available: No

Price Category: H

Images provided by designer/architect.

CAD FILE AVAILABLE

Rear View

Copyright by designer/architect.

Images provided by designer/architect.

Plan #F01-351102

Dimensions: 67' W x 56' D
Levels: 1
Heated Square Footage: 2,000
Bedrooms: 3
Bathrooms: 2½
Foundation: Crawl space, slab or basement
Materials List Available: Yes
Price Category: I

Rear View

Copyright by designer/architect.

Images provided by designer/architect.

Plan #F01-441008

Dimensions: 60' W x 50' D
Levels: 1
Heated Square Footage: 2,001
Bedrooms: 3
Bathrooms: 2
Foundation: Crawl space; slab or basement available for fee
Materials List Available: No
Price Category: F

1,501–2,500 sq. ft.

Plan #F01-211048

Images provided by designer/architect.

Dimensions: 66' W x 60' D

Levels: 1

Heated Square Footage: 2,002

Bedrooms: 3

Bathrooms: 2

Foundation: Crawl space; slab or basement for fee

Materials List Available: Yes

Price Category: D

Copyright by designer/architect.

Plan #F01-221018

Images provided by designer/architect.

Dimensions: 67' W x 53' D

Levels: 1

Heated Square Footage: 2,007

Bedrooms: 3

Bathrooms: 2

Foundation: Basement

Materials List Available: No

Price Category: D

Copyright by designer/architect.

Rear Elevation

Copyright by designer/architect.

Bonus Area

Plan #F01-351069

Dimensions: 78' W x 49'6" D

Levels: 1

Heated Square Footage: 2,008

Bedrooms: 3

Bathrooms: 2½

Foundation: Crawl space, basement or slab

Materials List Available: Yes

Price Category: H

Images provided by designer/architect.

CAD FILE AVAILABLE

Plan #F01-241007

Dimensions: 58'10" W x 59'1" D

Levels: 1

Heated Square Footage: 2,036

Bedrooms: 3

Bathrooms: 2

Foundation: Crawl space or slab

Materials List Available: No

Price Category: D

Images provided by designer/architect.

Bonus Area

Plan #F01-321030

Dimensions: 61' W x 51' D
Levels: 1
Heated Square Footage: 2,029
Bedrooms: 4
Bathrooms: 2
Foundation: Crawl space, slab
or basement
Materials List Available: Yes
Price Category: F

CAD FILE AVAILABLE

Images provided by designer/architect.

Two covered porches and a rear patio make this lovely home fit right into a site with a view.

Features:

- Great Room: Boxed entryway columns, a vaulted ceiling, a corner fireplace, a windowed wall, and door to the patio are highlights of this spacious room.

- Study: Tucked into the back of the house for privacy, the study also opens to the rear patio.

- Dining Area: The windowed alcove lets natural light flow into this room, which adjoins the kitchen.

- Kitchen: A central island, deep pantry, and ample counter area make this room a cook's delight.

- Master Suite: You'll love the two walk-in closets, decorative bedroom window, and double doors opening to the private porch. The bath includes a garden tub, a separate shower, and two vanities.

- Additional Bedrooms: Both bedrooms have a walk-in closet.

Plan #F01-151105

Dimensions: 60'6" W x 91'4" D

Levels: 1

Heated Square Footage: 2,039

Bedrooms: 4

Bathrooms: 2

Foundation: Crawl space or slab; basement for fee or optional basement

Materials List Available: No

Price Category: I

Images provided by designer/architect.

If you've always wanted a wraparound porch with columns, this could be your dream home.

Features:

- **Great Room:** Just off the foyer, this spacious room features a handsome fireplace where friends and family are sure to gather.

- **Dining Room:** Columns set off this dining room, and the large window area allows natural lighting during the day.

- **Kitchen:** Open to the dining room, this well-planned kitchen features a large central island with a sink and a dishwasher on one side and an eating bar on the other.

- **Breakfast Room:** You'll love the unusual shape of this room and its windows overlooking the rear porch. Access to the porch is from a hallway here.

- **Master Suite:** Enjoy two walk-in closets, plus a bath with a corner whirlpool tub, a glass shower, a linen closet, vanity, and compartmentalized toilet.

Copyright by designer/architect.

Bonus Area

Plan #F01-761047

Dimensions: 60' W x 70' D

Levels: 1

Heated Square Footage: 1,983

Bedrooms: 3

Bathrooms: 2

Foundation: Basement

Materials List Available: Yes

Price Category: D

Multiple dormers and gables add plenty of character to the exterior of this home.

Features:

- Kitchen: The kitchen overlooks the breakfast area and great room, providing an open atmosphere.

- Breakfast Room: The vaulted breakfast area includes direct access to the outdoor patio, while the vaulted great room offers patio views.

- Master Suite: The master bedroom becomes a private oasis for the homeowners and features a tranquil bath with a soothing corner whirlpool tub and a large walk-in closet.

Images provided by designer/architect.

Plan #F01-101030

Dimensions: 63' W x 63' D
Levels: 1
Heated Square Footage: 2,071
Bedrooms: 3
Bathrooms: 2½
Foundation: Crawl space or basement
Materials List Available: No
Price Category: F

This lovely three-bedroom brick home with an optional bonus room above the three-car garage is just what you've been looking for.

Features:

- **Family Room:** This large room, with its high ceiling and cozy fireplace, is great for entertaining.

- **Kitchen:** This kitchen boasts a built-in pantry and a peninsula opening into the breakfast nook.

- **Master Suite:** This suite, with its 14-ft.-high ceiling and private sitting area, is a perfect place to relax after a long day. The bath has a double-bowl vanity, large walk-in closet, and soaking tub.

- **Bedrooms:** Two additional bedrooms feature walk-in closets and share a private bathroom.

Plan #F01-351105

Dimensions: 69' W x 59'10" D
Levels: 1
Heated Square Footage: 2,000
Bedrooms: 3
Bathrooms: 2½
Foundation: Crawl space or slab
Materials List Available: Yes
Price Category: I

Images provided by designer/architect.

This inviting home has rustic styling with upscale features.

Features:

- **Outdoor Living:** The front and rear covered porches add plenty of usable outdoor living space and include that much-requested outdoor kitchen.

- **Great Room:** This expansive great room includes a beautiful trayed ceiling and features built-in cabinets and a gas fireplace.

- **Kitchen:** This spacious kitchen features an oversize island with a large eating bar and breakfast area.

- **Master Suite:** The master bedroom has a raised ceiling and opens into the well-equipped bath that includes dual sinks, an oversized corner jet tub, and large double walk-in closets.

- **Flex Space:** There is a storage area off of the garage for projects and storage. The media/hobby space could be used as a home office, dining room, or playroom.

Kitchen

Master Bathroom

Outdoor Kitchen

Covered Porch 23-0 x 8-0

Patio

Garden Tub

M. Bath 15-4 x 9-6

9-0 Ceiling
10-0 Ceiling

Master Bedroom 14-0 x 15-6

Kitchen 11-6 x 15-6

Island Bar

Eating 11-2 x 15-6
9-0 Ceiling

Bedroom 2 13-4 x 11-6
9-0 Ceiling

S

Clos. 7-6 x 5-8

Clos. 7-6 x 5-8

Ref.

Pantry

Brm.

C

Stor. 8-5 x 7-4

WH

D

Utility 8-3 x 7-2

W

Entry

C

Half Bath

9-0 Ceiling
10-0 Ceiling

Great Room 22-8 x 15-6 (Clear)

Cabs

Gas Logs

Hall

Hall Bath

Lin.

L

C

Tub/ Shwr.

C

Sloped Clg. ↓

UP

Media/ Hobby 8-0 x 7-10

Cabs

2 Car Garage 23-4 x 23-10

Covered Porch 23-0 x 5-0

Bedroom 3 13-4 x 11-6
9-0 Ceiling

Copyright by designer/architect.

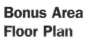

CH

S

LIN.

ATTIC ACCESS

ATTIC ACCESS

SLOPED CLG.

SLOPED CLG.

Unfinished Bonus Room 14-0 x 23-10 (Clear)
8-0 Clg. Ht.

Bonus Area Floor Plan

Rear View

Plan #F01-161026

Dimensions: 67'6" W x 63'6" D

Levels: 1

Heated Square Footage: 2,041

Bedrooms: 3

Bathrooms: 2

Foundation: Basement

Materials List Available: No

Price Category: D

Images provided by designer/architect.

Optional Basement Level

Copyright by designer/architect.

Plan #F01-351126

Dimensions: 69' W x 63'10" D

Levels: 1

Heated Square Footage: 2,021

Bedrooms: 3

Bathrooms: 2½

Foundation: Basement

Materials List Available: Yes

Price Category: H

Images provided by designer/architect.

Copyright by designer/architect.

Bonus Area

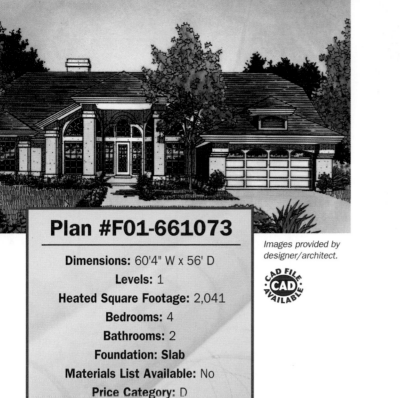

Floor plan labels:

Bedroom 4 13'⁴ · 9'⁴
Bath 2
Covered Patio
Master Suite 14'⁴ · 16'⁴
Bedroom 3 11'⁰ · 11'⁰
Nook
Family Rm. 18'⁴ · 14'⁴
w.i.c.
Kitchen
Master Bath
Bedroom 2 11'⁰ · 11'⁰
Living Rm. 10'¹⁰ · 13'²
Foyer
Dining Rm. 10'¹⁰ · 13'²
Laun.
Entry
2 Car Garage 20'⁰ · 20'⁰

Images provided by designer/architect.

Copyright by designer/architect.

Front View

Plan #F01-661073

Dimensions: 60'4" W x 56' D

Levels: 1

Heated Square Footage: 2,041

Bedrooms: 4

Bathrooms: 2

Foundation: Slab

Materials List Available: No

Price Category: D

CAD FILE AVAILABLE · CAD

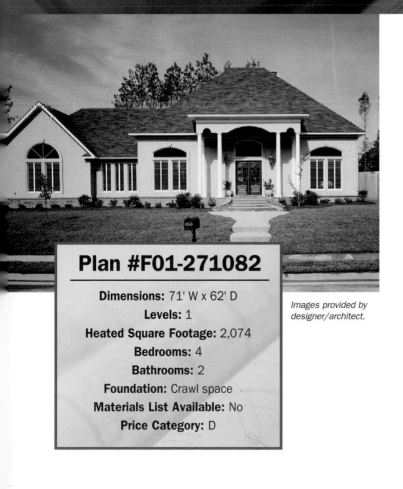

Plan #F01-271082

Dimensions: 71' W x 62' D

Levels: 1

Heated Square Footage: 2,074

Bedrooms: 4

Bathrooms: 2

Foundation: Crawl space

Materials List Available: No

Price Category: D

Images provided by designer/architect.

Copyright by designer/architect.

Floor plan labels:

GARAGE 21'-4"x21'-6"
PATIO
DECK
BEDRM 3 14'-0"x12'-0"
PORCH 2
BEDRM 4 9'-10"x12'-0"
STORAGE
MSTR BATH
UTIL
DINING 12'-0"x12'-4" 12'-0"clg
LIVING 17'-10"x20'-4" 12'-0"clg
BATH 2
MASTER BEDROOM 15'-0"x13'-4" 15'-0" cathedral clg
EATING 10'-4"x11'-4"
KITCH 11'-4"x12'-4" 12'-0"clg
FOYER
BEDRM 2 14'-2"x11'-4" 12'-0"clg
PORCH 1

Copyright by
designer/architect.

Images provided by
designer/architect.

Kitchen Views

Plan #F01-761002

Dimensions: 68'4" W x 56' D
Levels: 1
Heated Square Footage: 2,241
Bedrooms: 4
Bathrooms: 2½
Foundation: Basement
Materials List Available: Yes
Price Category: C

1,501–2,500 sq. ft.

Copyright by designer/architect.

Plan #F01-101008

Dimensions: 68' W x 53' D
Levels: 1
Heated Square Footage: 2,088
Bedrooms: 3
Bathrooms: 2½
Foundation: Crawl space, slab, or basement
Materials List Available: Yes
Price Category: H

Images provided by designer/architect.

SMARTtip
Accentuating Your Bathroom with Details

No matter how big or small the room, details will pull the style together. Some of the best details that you can include are the smallest—drawer pulls from an antique store or shells in a glass jar or just left on the countertop. Add period flavor with crown molding, or dress up contemporary fixtures with polished stone fittings.

Plan #F01-171015

Images provided by designer/architect.

Dimensions: 79' W x 46' D
Levels: 1
Heated Square Footage: 2,089
Bedrooms: 3
Bathrooms: 2½
Foundation: Crawl space or slab
Materials List Available: Yes
Price Category: D

Bonus Area

Plan #F01-191032

Images provided by designer/architect.

Dimensions: 80'4" W x 52' D
Levels: 1
Heated Square Footage: 2,091
Bedrooms: 3
Bathrooms: 2
Foundation: Slab or crawl space
Materials List Available: No
Price Category: F

Choosing Kitchen Cabinets

Who can't relate to this scenario: you turn on the oven to preheat it, but wait, did you take out the large roasting pan first? How about the lasagna dish, muffin tins, pizza stone, and cookie sheets that are in there, too? Now where can you put everything that was in the oven while the casserole is baking, and the countertop is laden with the rest of tonight's dinner ingredients?

The oven, it seems, has become the catch-all for the big, awkward stuff that you can't fit into kitchen cabinets but is just too ugly to display. Besides, the countertop is where you keep the toaster oven, food processor, coffeemaker, canisters, hand mixer, portable TV, notepad, coupon file, bills, hand lotion, car keys, and your vitamins! Wouldn't life be grand if there was a place for everything and everything was in its place?

Good cabinetry outfitted with an assortment of organizing options can help you there. It can make your kitchen more efficient and a whole lot neater while establishing a style, or "look," for the room. Keep in mind, however, that cabinetry will also consume about 40 percent of your kitchen design budget, according to the NKBA. So before making any expensive decisions — or costly mistakes — investigate all of the various cabinetry options that are available to you.

Cabinet Construction

Basically, cabinets are constructed in one of two ways: framed or frameless. Framed cabinets have a traditional look, with a full frame across the face of the cabinet box that may show between closed doors. This secures adjacent cabinets and strengthens wider cabinet boxes with a center rail. Hinges on framed cabinets may or may not be visible around doors when they are closed. The door's face may be ornamented with raised or recessed panels, trimmed or framed panels, or a framed-glass panel with or without muntins (the narrow vertical and horizontal strips of wood that divide panes of glass).

Frameless cabinets — also known as European-style cabinets, although American manufacturers also make them — are built without a face frame and sport a clean, contemporary look. There's no trim or molding with this simple design. Close-fitting doors cover the entire front of the box; no ornamentation appears on the face of the doors; and hinges are typically hidden inside the cabinet box.

Choosing one type over another is generally a matter of taste, although framed units offer slightly less interior space. But the quality of construction is a factor that should always be taken into consideration. How do you judge it? Solid wood is too expensive for most of today's budgets, but it might be used on just the doors and frames. More typical is plywood box construction, which offers good structural support and solid wood on the doors and frames. To save money, cabinetmakers sometimes use strong plywood for support elements, such as the box and frame, and medium-density fiberboard for other parts, such as doors and drawer fronts. In yet another alternative, good-quality laminate cabinets can be made with high-quality, thick particleboard underneath the laminate finish.

There are other things to look for in cabinet construction. They include dovetail or mortise-and-tenon joinery and solidly mortised hinges. Also, make sure that the interior of every cabinet is well finished, with adjustable shelves that are a minimum ⅝ inch thick to prevent bowing.

Unless you have the time and skill to build the cabinets yourself or can hire someone else to do it, you'll have to purchase them in one of four ways. Knockdown cabinetry (also known as RTA, ready to assemble) is shipped flat and, sometimes, unfinished because you put the pieces together. Stock cabinetry comes in standard sizes but limited styles and colors; it is often available on the spot or can be delivered quickly. Like stock, semi-custom cabinetry comes in standard styles, but it is manufactured to fit a homeowner's specific size and finish needs. Custom cabinetry is not limited in terms of style or size because it is built to the designer's specifications.

Cabinet Accessories & Options

Most people would agree that no matter how much storage space they have, they need even more. The problem often isn't the amount, it's the inaccessible placement and inefficient configuration of the storage space. One of the greatest benefits today's designers and manufacturers offer is fitted and accessorized interiors that maximize even the smallest nook and cranny inside cabinets and drawers. These accommodations not

Color makes all the difference in a room. Here, a variety of creamy colors throughout the kitchen adds personality. Pretty green and blue cabinets are a nice change from plain white.

An updated country style, cabinets with sleeker lines and elegant granite counters intermingle here with the usual down-home charm and informal mix of woods and hardware.

only expand the use of space, but increase convenience and accessibility. Among them are the following:

Appliance Garages. Appliance garages make use of dead space in a corner, but they can be installed anywhere in the vertical space between the wall-mounted cabinet and the countertop. A tambour (rolltop) door hides small appliances such as a food processor or anything else you want within reach but hidden from view. This form of minicabinet can be equipped with an electrical outlet and can even be divided into separate sections to store more than one item. Reserve part of the appliance garage for cookbook storage, or outfit it with small drawers for little items or spices. Customize an appliance garage any way you like.

Lazy Susans and Carousel Shelves. These rotating shelves maximize dead corner storage and put items such as dishes or pots and pans within easy reach. A Lazy Susan rotates 360 degrees, so just spin it to find what you're looking for. Carousel shelves, which attach to two right-angled doors, rotate 270 degrees; open the doors and the shelves, which are actually attached to the doors, put any item within hand reach. Pivoting shelves are a variation on the carousel design and may or may not be door-mounted. In addition, units may be built into taller cabinets, creating a pantry that can store a lot in a small amount of space.

Fold-Down Mixer Shelf. This spring-loaded shelf swings up and out of a base cabinet for use, then folds down and back

These custom cabinets add unique options, such as pullout storage for dish linens and angled cabinets that make use of small spaces.

into the cabinet when the mixer is no longer needed, which reduces clutter by keeping the countertop clear of appliances.

Slide-Outs and Tilt-Outs. Installed in base cabinets, slide-out trays and racks store small appliances, linens, cans, or boxed items, while slide-out bins are good for holding onions, potatoes, grains, pet food, or potting soil — even garbage or recycling containers. A tilt-out tray is located in the often-wasted area just below the lip of the countertop in front of the sink and above base cabinet doors. It looks like a drawer but tilts open to provide a neat nook for sponges and scouring pads that look messy when left on the counter.

Built-in Pantry Units. These fold-out or slide-out units can be fitted into narrow areas that might otherwise remain wasted. Store dry or canned goods here. Fold-out units have door-mounted shelves and an in-cabinet shelf that pivots; slide-out units fit multiple shelves in a cabinet.

In addition to these options, check out everything that a cabinet manufacturer has to offer to make the most of a cabinet's storage capacity. Other items to look for include special racks for trays and cookie sheets, drawer inserts for organizing spices and utensils, watertight recycling bins, wine racks, fold-down recipe book rests, sliding pot racks, built-in canister drawers, and plate racks.

Unique two-toned cabinetry adds interest in a country kitchen, left. The appliances are integrated with the same two-toned panels and the hardware echoes the geometric design.

Glass-fronted bins are a colorful and convenient way to store pasta and dried beans, opposite bottom left.

Personalize your kitchen with cabinets made from exotic wood and finished with a custom-mixed high-gloss lacquer, opposite bottom right.

Cabinetry with the look of fine furniture integrates this kitchen almost seamlessly into an adjacent living space, below.

If you decide to add cabinets without a lot of built-ins, consider refitting them with cabinet organizers. These plastic, plastic-coated wire, or enameled-steel racks and hangers are widely available at department stores and home centers.

Beware of the temptation to over-specialize your kitchen storage. Sizes and needs for certain items change, so be sure to allot at least 50 percent of your kitchen's storage to standard cabinets with one or more movable shelves.

The Decorative Role of Cabinets

The look you create in your kitchen will be largely influenced by the cabinetry you select. Finding a style that suits you and how you will use your new kitchen is similar to shopping for furniture. In fact, don't be surprised to see many furniture details dressing up the cabinets on view in showrooms and home centers today.

Besides architectural elements such as fluted pilasters, corbels, moldings, and bull's-eye panels, look for details such as fretwork, rope motifs, gingerbread trim, balusters, composition ornamentation (it looks like carving), even footed cabinets that mimic freestanding furniture pieces.

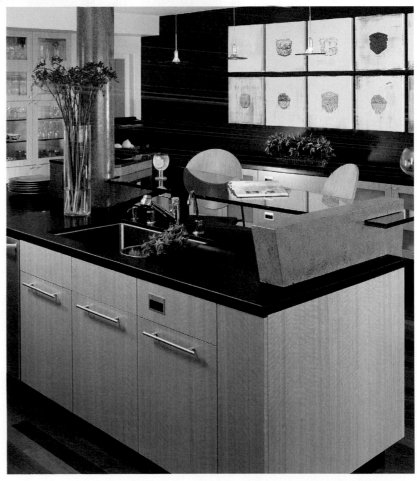

If your taste runs toward less-fussy design, you'll also find handsome door and drawer styles that feature minimal or no decoration. Woods and finishes are just as varied, and range from informal looks in birch, oak, ash, and maple to rich mahogany and cherry. Laminate finishes, though less popular than they were a decade ago, haven't completely disappeared from the marketplace, but an array of colors has replaced the once-ubiquitous almond and white finishes.

Color

Color is coming on strong on wood cabinetry, too. Accents in one, two, or more hues are pairing with natural wood tones. White-painted cabinets take on a warmer glow with tinted shades of this always popular neutral. Special "vintage" finishes, such as translucent color glazes, continue to grow in popularity, as do distressed finishing techniques, such as wire brushing and rubbed-through color that add both another dimension and the appeal of handcraftmanship, even on mass-produced items. Contemporary kitchens, which historically favor an all-white palette, are warming up with earthier neutral shades, less sterile off-whites, and wood.

If you're shy about using color on such a high-ticket item as cabinetry, try it as an accent on molding, door trim, or island cabinetry. Just as matched furniture suites have become passé in other rooms of the house, the same is true for the kitchen, where mixing several looks can add sophistication and visual interest.

Hardware

Another way to emphasize your kitchen's decorative style is
with hardware. From exquisite reproductions in brass, pewter,
wrought iron, or ceramic to handsome bronze, chrome,
nickel, glass, steel, plastic, rubber, wood, or stone creations, a
smorgasbord of shapes and designs is available. Some pieces are
highly polished; others are matte-finished, smooth, or hammered.
Some are abstract or geometrical; others are simple, elegant
shapes. Whimsical designs take on the forms of animals or
teapots, vegetables or flowers. Even just one or two great-looking
door or drawer pulls can be showstoppers in a kitchen that may
otherwise be devoid of much personality. Like mixing cabinet
finishes, a combination of two hardware styles — perhaps
picked up from other materials in the room — makes a big
design statement. As the famed architect Mies Van der Rohe
once stated, "God is in the details," and the most perfect detail
in your new kitchen may be the artistic hardware that you select.

Besides looks, consider the function of a pull or knob. You
have to be able to grip it easily and comfortably. If your fingers
or hands get stiff easily, select C- or U-shaped pulls. If you like a
knob, try it out in the showroom to make sure it isn't slippery or
awkward when you grab it. Knobs and pulls can be inexpensive
if you can stick to unfinished ones that you can paint in an
accent color picked up from the tile or wallpaper. If you want to
save money at first, you can start with simple knobs and pulls
and change them later. Replacing the hardware can redefine the
style of the cabinets. The right knob or pull can suggest any one
of a number of vintage looks or decorative styles.

This cabinet color, opposite, was chosen to echo one of the
colors in the granite countertop and backsplash.

Satin-finish hardware looks great against paint with a soft
metallic sheen, while the center of each handle reflects the
granite countertop, top left.

Unique braided handles personalize plain cabinetry, top right.

The homeowner matched this pattern in the adjacent
accessories. Adding natural-wood accents, such as these drawer
handles, helps balance the traditional and modern styles that
are both in play in this kitchen, below.

Images provided by designer/architect.

Plan #F01-151050

Dimensions: 69'2" W x 74'10" D
Levels: 1
Heated Square Footage: 2,096
Bedrooms: 3
Bathrooms: 2½
Foundation: Crawl space or slab, basement or walkout for fee
Materials List Available: No
Price Category: J

You'll love this spacious home for both its elegance and its convenient design.

Features:

- Ceiling Height: 8 ft.

- Great Room: A 9-ft. boxed ceiling complements this large room, which sits just beyond the front gallery. A fireplace and door to the rear porch make it a natural gathering spot.

- Kitchen: This well-designed kitchen includes a central work island and shares an angled eating bar with the adjacent breakfast room.

- Breakfast Room: This room's bay window is gorgeous, and the door to the garage is practical.

- Master Suite: You'll love the 9-ft. boxed ceiling in the bedroom and the vaulted ceiling in the bath, which also includes two walk-in closets, a whirlpool tub, split vanities, a shower, and a separate toilet room.

- Workshop: A hugh workshop with a half-bath is ideal for anyone who loves to build or repair.

Bathroom

Kitchen

Master Bedroom

Images provided by designer/architect.

Plan #F01-151850

Dimensions: 66' W x 52' D
Levels: 1
Heated Square Footage: 2,075
Bedrooms: 4
Bathrooms: 3
Foundation: Crawl space or slab; basement or walkout for fee
Materials List Available: No
Price Category: J

This European-style home has beautiful details both inside and outside.

Features:

- Courtyard: Upon walking up the path to the entry of this home, you are greeted by a courtyard, where you can plant flowers and set up an area to relax in the sun.

- Great Room: Entertain your friends and family in this great room, which features access to the grilling porch at the rear of the home, a fireplace, and a connection to the kitchen.

- Kitchen: This kitchen was created with many wonderful details, including a pantry, an eating bar, and an attached breakfast room.

- Master Suite: Featuring access to the grilling porch, a spacious walk-in closet, a dual-sink vanity, and a whirlpool tub, this master suite is a great place to relax after a long day.

Copyright by designer/architect.

Plan #F01-101009

Dimensions: 70'2" W x 59' D
Levels: 1
Heated Square Footage: 2,097
Bedrooms: 3
Bathrooms: 3
Foundation: Crawl space, slab, or basement
Materials List Available: Yes
Price Category: H

Round columns enhance this country porch design, which will nestle into any neighborhood.

Features:

- Ceiling Height: 9 ft. unless otherwise noted.

- Family Room: This large family room seems even more spacious, thanks to the vaulted ceiling. It's the perfect spot for all kinds of family activities.

- Dining Room: This elegant dining room is adorned with a decorative round column and a tray ceiling.

- Kitchen: You'll love the convenience of this enormous 14-ft.-3-in. x 22-ft.-6-in. country kitchen, which is open to the family room.

- Screened Porch: A French door leads to this breezy porch, with its vaulted ceiling.

- Master Suite: This sumptuous suite includes a double tray ceiling, a sitting area, a large walk-in closet, and a luxurious bath.

- Patio or Deck: This area is accessible from both the screened porch and master suite.

Images provided by designer/architect.

This home, as shown in the photograph, may differ from the actual blueprints. For more detailed information, please check floor plans carefully.

Single-Level Decks

A single-level deck can use a strong vertical element, such as a pergola or a gazebo, to make it interesting. A simple and less-expensive option is a potted conical shrub or a clematis growing on a trellis.

Plan #F01-151703

Dimensions: 69'2" W x 74'10" D

Levels: 1

Heated Square Footage: 2,096

Bedrooms: 3

Bathrooms: 2½

Foundation: Crawl space or slab; basement or walkout for fee

Materials List Available: No

Price Category: J

Images provided by designer/architect.

CAD FILE AVAILABLE

Main Level

Optional Foundation

Bonus Area Floor Plan

Plan #F01-351053

Dimensions: 79'4" W x 53'6" D

Levels: 1

Heated Square Footage: 2,100

Bedrooms: 3

Bathrooms: 3

Foundation: Crawl space, slab or basement

Materials List Available: Yes

Price Category: I

Images provided by designer/architect.

CAD FILE AVAILABLE

Plan #F01-151004

Dimensions: 64'8" W x 62'1" D

Levels: 1

Heated Square Footage: 2,107

Bedrooms: 4

Bathrooms: 2½

Foundation: Crawl space or slab; basement for fee

Materials List Available: Yes

Price Category: I

Images provided by designer/architect.

This home, as shown in the photograph, may differ from the actual blueprints. For more detailed information, please check floor plans carefully.

Copyright by designer/architect.

Plan #F01-161092

Dimensions: 92'6" W x 56'8" D

Levels: 1

Heated Square Footage: 2,110

Bedrooms: 3

Bathrooms: 2

Foundation: Walkout; basement, crawl space or slab for fee

Materials List Available: Yes

Price Category: D

Images provided by designer/architect.

Optional Lower Level

Plan #F01-151495

Dimensions: 67'2" W x 64'8" D

Levels: 1

Heated Square Footage: 2,121

Bedrooms: 3

Bathrooms: 2

Foundation: Slab; basement for fee

Materials List Available: No

Price Category: H

Images provided by designer/architect.

CAD FILE AVAILABLE

Plan #F01-191055

Dimensions: 60' W x 76' D

Levels: 1

Heated Square Footage: 2,123

Bedrooms: 3

Bathrooms: 2½

Foundation: Crawl space or slab

Materials List Available: No

Price Category: E

Images provided by designer/architect.

Plan #F01-501723

Dimensions: 101'9" W x 63'9" D
Levels: 1
Heated Square Footage: 2,125
Bedrooms: 2
Bathrooms: 2
Foundation: Crawl space
Materials List Available: No
Price Category: D

Images provided by designer/architect.

CAD FILE AVAILABLE

Copyright by designer/architect.

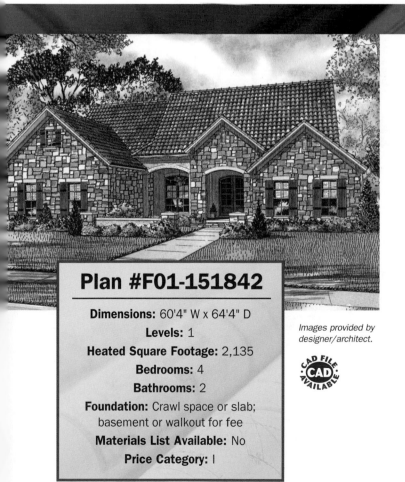

Plan #F01-151842

Dimensions: 60'4" W x 64'4" D
Levels: 1
Heated Square Footage: 2,135
Bedrooms: 4
Bathrooms: 2
Foundation: Crawl space or slab; basement or walkout for fee
Materials List Available: No
Price Category: I

Images provided by designer/architect.

CAD FILE AVAILABLE

Bonus Area

Copyright by designer/architect.

Plan #F01-191012

Dimensions: 60' W x 76' D
Levels: 1
Heated Square Footage: 2,123
Bedrooms: 3
Bathrooms: 2½
Foundation: Crawl space or slab
Materials List Available: No
Price Category: F

The wraparound porch adds to the charm of this home.

Features:

- Porches: The front wraparound porch will be the perfect spot to greet neighbors as they stroll by. The rear porch is a private place to relax and enjoy a beautiful day.

- Great Room: This large gathering area features a 10-ft.-high ceiling and large windows, which offer a view of the backyard. There is even room for a formal dining table.

- Master Suite: Located on the opposite side of the home from the secondary bedrooms, this retreat offers a large sleeping area. The master bath will pamper you with an oversize shower, a tub, and a double-bowl vanity.

- Secondary Bedrooms: Two similarly sized bedrooms have ample closet space and share a full bathroom.

Images provided by designer/architect.

Kitchen

Copyright by designer/architect.

Images provided by designer/architect.

Plan #F01-151171

Dimensions: 63'10" W x 72'2" D

Levels: 1

Heated Square Footage: 2,131

Bedrooms: 3

Bathrooms: 2½

Foundation: Crawl space or slab; basement or walkout for fee

Materials List Available: No

Price Category: I

This home has everything an active family could possibly want — beauty, luxury, and plenty of space to relax and entertain, both inside and out.

Features:

- **Great Room:** Skylights in the vaulted ceiling, a fireplace, and the door to the rear screened porch make this a favorite place to spend time.

- **Dining Area:** Bay windows let light flood the area.

- **Kitchen:** The central island and snack bar, pantry, computer center, and ample counter and cabinet space make a great working area.

- **Storm Shelter:** You'll be happy to have this room, and even happier not to have to use it.

- **Master Suite:** The vaulted ceiling, door to the grilling patio, two walk-in closets, and luxury bath combine to create a suite you'll love.

- **Additional Bedrooms:** A window seat in one room is a child's dream, and you'll love the big closets.

Copyright by designer/architect.

Plan #F01-151034

Dimensions: 58'6" W x 64'6" D

Levels: 1

Heated Square Footage: 2,133

Bedrooms: 3

Bathrooms: 2

Foundation: Crawl space or slab; basement or walkout for fee

Materials List Available: No

Price Category: H

This home, as shown in the photograph, may differ from the actual blueprints. For more detailed information, please check the floor plans carefully.

Images provided by designer/architect.

You'll love the high ceilings, open floor plan, and contemporary design features in this home.

Features:

- Great Room: A pass-through tiled fireplacebetween this lovely large room and the adjacent hearth room allows you to notice the mirror effect created by the 10-ft. boxed ceilings in both rooms.

- Dining Room: An 11-ft. ceiling and 8-in. boxed column give formality to this lovely room, where you're certain to entertain.

- Kitchen: If you're a cook, this room may become your favorite spot in the house, thanks to its great design, which includes plenty of work and storage space, and a very practical layout.

- Master Suite: A 10-ft. boxed ceiling gives elegance to this room. A pocket door opens to the private bath, with its huge walk-in closet, glass-blocked whirlpool tub, separate glass shower, and private toilet room.

Rendering reflects floor plan

Plan #F01-101011

Dimensions: 71'2" W x 58'1" D
Levels: 1
Heated Square Footage: 2,184
Bedrooms: 3
Bathrooms: 3
Foundation: Crawl space, slab, basement, or walkout
Materials List Available: Yes
Price Category: H

A classic design and spacious interior add up to a flexible design suitable to any modern lifestyle.

Features:

- Ceiling Height: 9 ft. unless otherwise noted.

- Dining Room: A decorative square column and a tray ceiling adorn this elegant dining room.

- Screened Porch: Enjoy summer breezes in style by stepping out of the French doors into this vaulted screened porch.

- Kitchen: Does everyone want to hang out in the kitchen while you are cooking? No problem. True to the home's country style, this huge 14-ft.-3-in. x 22-ft.-6-in. kitchen has plenty of room for helpers. This area is open to the vaulted family room.

- Patio or Deck: This pleasant outdoor area is accessible from both the screened porch and the master bedroom.

- Master Suite: This luxurious suite includes a double tray ceiling, a sitting area, two walk-in closets, and an exquisite bath.

CAD FILE AVAILABLE

Kitchen

Copyright by designer/architect.

Plan #F01-351206

Dimensions: 71' W x 77' D

Levels: 1

Heated Square Footage: 2,140

Bedrooms: 4

Bathrooms: 2½

Foundation: Crawl space, slab or basement

Materials List Available: Yes

Price Category: H

Images provided by designer/architect.

CAD FILE AVAILABLE

Bonus Area

Bonus Room
14-0 x 33-4

Bedroom 4
11-4 x 11-6

Covered Porch
23-0 x 8-0

Kitchen
11-6 x 15-6

Master Bath
15-4 x 9-6

Bedroom 3
11-4 x 11-2

Eating Area
11-2 x 15-6

Master Bedroom
14-0 x 15-6

Closet
7-6 x 5-8

Closet
7-6 x 5-8

Bedroom 2
11-4 x 11-4

Great Room
22-8 x 15-6
(Clear)

Laundry
8-4 x 7-8

Storage

Media / Hobby
8-0 x 7-10

Workshop
19-2 x 10-4

Covered Porch
23-4 x 7-0

Two Car Garage
23-4 x 22-8

Copyright by designer/architect.

Plan #F01-351071

Dimensions: 51'8" W x 59' D

Levels: 1

Heated Square Footage: 1,600

Bedrooms: 3

Bathrooms: 2

Foundation: Basement

Materials List Available: Yes

Price Category: H

Images provided by designer/architect.

Dining or Sunroom
12 x 18-6
9' Ceiling

Rear Porch
7 x 14-2

Patio
14-8 x 14-2

Bedroom 1
11-6 x 13
9' Ceiling

Master Bedroom
16 x 12-8

Kitchen
12 x 12

Bath

Great Room
17-6 x 15
(Clear)

Bedroom 2
11-6 x 13
9' Ceiling

Two Car Garage
21-4 x 21-4
(Clear)

Front Porch
17-6 x 5-0

Copyright by designer/architect.

Images provided by designer/architect.

Copyright by designer/architect.

Front View

Plan #F01-191001

Dimensions: 62' W x 72' D

Levels: 1

Heated Square Footage: 2,156

Bedrooms: 4

Bathrooms: 3

Foundation: Crawl space, slab, or basement

Materials List Available: No

Price Category: F

Images provided by designer/architect.

Copyright by designer/architect.

Plan #F01-121117

Dimensions: 76' W x 46' D

Levels: 1

Heated Square Footage: 2,172

Bedrooms: 4

Bathrooms: 3

Foundation: Basement; crawl space for fee

Materials List Available: Yes

Price Category: D

Plan #F01-191009

Dimensions: 62' W x 76' D

Levels: 1

Heated Square Footage: 2,172

Bedrooms: 4

Bathrooms: 2

Foundation: Crawl space or slab

Materials List Available: No

Price Category: F

Images provided by designer/architect.

This charming home is equally attractive in a rural or a settled area, thanks to its classic lines.

Features:

- Porches: Covered front and back porches emphasize the comfort you'll find in this home.

- Great Room: A tray ceiling gives elegance to this spacious room, where everyone is sure to gather. A fireplace makes a nice focal point, and French doors open onto the rear covered porch.

- Dining Room: Arched openings give distinction to this room, where it's easy to serve meals for the family or host a large group.

- Kitchen: You'll love the cooktop island, walk-in pantry, wall oven, snack bar, and view out of the windows in the adjoining breakfast area.

- Master Suite: The large bedroom here gives you space to spread out and relax, and the bath includes a corner whirlpool tub, shower, and dual sinks. An 8-ft. x 10-ft. walk-in closet is off of the bath.

Copyright by designer/architect.

Plan #F01-271076

Dimensions: 69' W x 57' D

Levels: 1

Heated Square Footage: 2,188

Bedrooms: 1

Bathrooms: 1½

Foundation: Walkout basement

Materials List Available: No

Price Category: D

This stunning home, with its optional finished basement plan to add two more bedrooms, would be perfect for your growing family.

Features:

- **Great Room:** This room with tray ceiling has a fireplace with built-in cabinets on either side.

- **Kitchen:** This island kitchen, with dinette area, is open to the great room.

- **Master Bedroom:** This room features a tray ceiling and a view of the backyard.

- **Master Bath:** This private bath has a walk-in closet and double vanities.

Images provided by designer/architect.

Optional Basement Level

Plan #F01-391138

Dimensions: 76' W x 75' D
Levels: 1
Heated Square Footage: 2,194
Bedrooms: 3
Bathrooms: 2
Foundation: Crawl space or basement
Materials List Available: Yes
Price Category: D

A truly sensational layout! A beautiful brick courtyard and a swimming pool anchor this unusual design.

Features:

- Living Room: This area is the interior highlight of the home. The large, exciting space features a skylight and large windows that flood the room with light.

- Kitchen: This large U-shaped kitchen has a raised bar, which is open to the living room. A pocket door leads to the dining area.

- Master Suite: This private retreat is located in a wing of its own. The suite has access to the rear patio. The master bath features dual vanities and a glass shower.

- Bedrooms: Two bedrooms are located on the opposite side of the home to give those in the master suite privacy. The family room will act as a playroom for the kids.

Images provided by designer/architect.

Plan #F01-761001

Dimensions: 70'4" W x 42'8" D
Levels: 1
Heated Square Footage: 2,025
Bedrooms: 3
Bathrooms: 2½
Foundation: Basement
Materials List Available: Yes
Price Category: B

The elegant exterior of this home will enhance any neighborhood, while double dormers and gables add curb appeal.

Features:

- Great Room: The cozy great room enjoys a 42" wood-burning fireplace as the main focal point along with a vaulted ceiling and 12' wall.

- Kitchen: The vaulted kitchen has a versatile cooktop island with separate oven for great functionality.

- Dining Room: The dining room has decorative columns and beams along with a vaulted ceiling for added spaciousness.

- Master Bedroom: An elegant coffered ceiling tops the private master bedroom.

- Energy-Efficient Walls: This home has the option of 2x6 walls for an additional fee. This makes a home more insulated, which results in lower heating and cooling bills.

Plan #F01-151113

Dimensions: 62'10" W x 91'4" D

Levels: 1

Heated Square Footage: 2,186

Bedrooms: 4

Bathrooms: 3

Foundation: Crawl space or slab; basement or walkout for fee

Materials List Available: No

Price Category: H

Images provided by designer/architect.

The porch on this four-bedroom ranch welcomes you home.

Features:

- Great Room: You'll find this large room just off the foyer.

- Dining Room: This room, with a view of the side yard, is located adjacent to the kitchen and the great room.

- Kitchen: This island kitchen, with a built-in pantry, is open to the breakfast area.

- Master Suite: This suite features double walk-in closets and a private bathroom with a double-bowl vanity and whirlpool tub.

- Bedrooms: Three secondary bedrooms have large closets and share a hall bathroom.

Optional Bonus Area

Copyright by designer/architect.

Plan #F01-131019

Dimensions: 83'6" W x 53'4" D

Levels: 1

Heated Square Footage: 2,243

Bedrooms: 3

Bathrooms: 2½

Foundation: Crawl space or slab; basement or walkout for fee

Materials List Available: Yes

Price Category: F

Drama marks this contemporary, angled ranch-style home which can be placed to suit any site, even the most difficult.

Images provided by designer/architect.

Features:

- **Great Room:** Imagine having an octagon-shaped great room! The shape alone makes it spectacular, but the view to the backyard from its four exterior sides adds to the impression it creates, and you'll love its 16-ft. tray ceiling, fireplace, and wall designed to fit a large entertainment center.

- **Kitchen:** This room is adjacent to and visually connected to the great room but has excellent features of its own that make it an easy place to cook or clean.

- **Master Suite:** Separated from the other bedrooms, this suite is planned for privacy. You'll love the bath here and look forward to the quiet you can find at the end of the day.

- **Additional Bedrooms:** In a wing of their own, the other two bedrooms share a bath.

Great Room

Rear Elevation

Plan #F01-161115

Dimensions: 79'8" W x 44'2" D
Levels: 1
Heated Square Footage: 2,253
Bedrooms: 4
Bathrooms: 3
Foundation: Walkout
Materials List Available: Yes
Price Category: E

This one-level home offers a beautiful exterior of brick and stone with shake siding.

Images provided by designer/architect.

Features:

- **Great Room:** This open gathering area features an 11-foot-high ceiling and access to the rear yard. Turn on the corner gas fireplace, and fill the room with warmth and charm.

- **Kitchen:** This peninsula kitchen with built-in pantry and counter seating offers easy access to both formal and informal dining. The laundry room and the garage are just a few steps away. A magnificent bay window decorates the breakfast room and brings natural light into the area.

- **Master Suite:** This retreat offers a furniture alcove in the sleeping area and a walk-in closet. The private bath features a double-bowl vanity and a whirlpool tub.

- **Guest Suite:** This private bedroom suite is located behind the three-car garage and offers a welcoming environment for your overnight guests.

- **Basement:** This full walkout basement expands the living space of the delightful home.

Left Elevation

Right Elevation

Rear Elevation

Images provided by designer/architect.

Plan #F01-171004

Dimensions: 72' W x 52' D
Levels: 1
Heated Square Footage: 2,256
Bedrooms: 3
Bathrooms: 2
Foundation: Crawl space or slab
Materials List Available: Yes
Price Category: E

This home greets you with a front porch featuring a high roofline and stucco columns.

Features:

- Ceiling Height: 9 ft. unless otherwise noted.

- Foyer: Step through the front porch into this impressive foyer, which opens to the formal dining room and the study.

- Dining Room: This dining room's 12 ft. ceiling enhances its sense of spaciousness,   with plenty of room for large dinner parties.

- Family Room: With plenty of room for all kinds of family activities, this room also has a 12-ft. ceiling, a fireplace, and two paddle fans.

- Kitchen: This kitchen has all the counter space you'll need to prepare your favorite recipes. There's a pantry, desk, and angled snack bar.

- Master Bedroom: This master retreat is separate from the other bedrooms for added privacy. It has an elegant, high step-up ceiling and a paddle fan.

- Master Bath: This master bath features a large walk-in closet, deluxe corner bath, walk-in shower, and a double-bowl vanity.

SMARTtip

Windows – Privacy

You can easily stencil a work of art onto a windowpane, perhaps only as a border around the edge. Choose or create a design that gives you as little or as much privacy and light control as you need. Use a ready-made stencil or a piece of openwork fabric such as lace, or mask a design onto the glass using tape and a razor knife. Then apply glass paint or frosted glass spray, referring to the instructions and guidelines that come with the product.

Copyright by designer/architect.

Plan #F01-111015

Dimensions: 64' W x 58' D

Levels: 1

Heated Square Footage: 2,208

Bedrooms: 4

Bathrooms: 2

Foundation: Slab

Materials List Available: No

Price Category: F

Images provided by designer/architect.

Copyright by designer/architect.

Plan #F01-121034

Dimensions: 92'8" W x 59'4" D

Levels: 1

Heated Square Footage: 2,223

Bedrooms: 1

Bathrooms: 1½

Foundation: Basement; crawl space for fee

Materials List Available: Yes

Price Category: E

Images provided by designer/architect.

Copyright by designer/architect.

Optional Basement Level

Copyright by designer/architect.

Plan #F01-271079

Dimensions: 104' W x 55' D

Levels: 1

Heated Square Footage: 2,228

Bedrooms: 1-3

Bathrooms: 1½

Foundation: Walkout basement

Materials List Available: No

Price Category: E

Images provided by designer/architect.

CAD FILE AVAILABLE

Optional Basement Level

Bonus Area

Plan #F01-371059

Dimensions: 77'8" W x 56'6" D

Levels: 1

Heated Square Footage: 2,240

Bedrooms: 4

Bathrooms: 2½

Foundation: Slab; crawl space for fee

Materials List Available: No

Price Category: E

Images provided by designer/architect.

CAD FILE AVAILABLE

Copyright by designer/architect.

Plan #F01-161249

Dimensions: 80'2" W x 51'8" D

Levels: 1

Heated Square Footage: 2,246

Bedrooms: 3

Bathrooms: 2

Foundation: Basement; crawl space, slab or walkout for fee

Materials List Available: Yes

Price Category: E

Images provided by designer/architect.

Copyright by designer/architect.

Plan #F01-351007

Dimensions: 73'8" W x 53'2" D

Levels: 1

Heated Square Footage: 2,251

Bedrooms: 3

Bathrooms: 2½

Foundation: Crawl space, slab, or basement

Materials List Available: Yes

Price Category: H

Images provided by designer/architect.

Copyright by designer/architect.

Bonus Area

Plan #F01-661160

Images provided by designer/architect.

CAD FILE AVAILABLE

Dimensions: 62'4" W x 57' D
Levels: 1
Heated Square Footage: 2,258
Bedrooms: 4
Bathrooms: 3
Foundation: Slab
Materials List Available: No
Price Category: F

Copyright by designer/architect.

Bonus Area

Plan #F01-101033

Images provided by designer/architect.

CAD FILE AVAILABLE

Dimensions: 62' W x 69'2" D
Levels: 1
Heated Square Footage: 2,260
Bedrooms: 3
Bathrooms: 3
Foundation: Basement
Materials List Available: No
Price Category: H

Copyright by designer/architect.

Plan #F01-761013

Dimensions: 65' W x 46'4" D

Levels: 1

Heated Square Footage: 1,562

Bedrooms: 3

Bathrooms: 2

Foundation: Basement

Materials List Available: Yes

Price Category: C

Images provided by designer/architect.

CAD FILE AVAILABLE

Plan #F01-121116

Dimensions: 72' W x 56' D

Levels: 1

Heated Square Footage: 2,276

Bedrooms: 3

Bathrooms: 2½

Foundation: Basement; crawl space for fee

Materials List Available: Yes

Price Category: E

Images provided by designer/architect.

Plan #F01-151634

Dimensions: 70' W x 73'8" D
Levels: 1
Heated Square Footage: 2,285
Bedrooms: 4
Bathrooms: 2
Foundation: Crawl space or slab
Materials List Available: No
Price Category: H

Images provided by designer/architect.

CAD FILE AVAILABLE

Copyright by designer/architect.

Plan #F01-761014

Dimensions: 96'6" W x 66' D
Levels: 1
Heated Square Footage: 2,487
Bedrooms: 3
Bathrooms: 2½
Foundation: Basement
Materials List Available: Yes
Price Category: E

Images provided by designer/architect.

CAD FILE AVAILABLE

Copyright by designer/architect.

Copyright by designer/architect.

DECK
19'-8" x 15'-0"

DINING
15'-10" x 11'-0"

HEARTH ROOM
16'-7" x 13'-0"

12' HIGH TRAY CEILING UP 1'

14' HIGH CEILING

MASTER BDRM
16'-0" x 15'-0"

FAMILY ROOM
16'-0" x 19'-0"

KITCHEN
16'-0" x 13'-0"

BRKFST
10'-0" x 10'-6"

STAIRS TO BONUS ROOM

BEDROOM 2
11'-0" x 14'-0"

BEDROOM 3
11'-0" x 14'-0"

ENTRY
12' HIGH CEILING

PORCH
12' HIGH CEILING

STAIRS TO BASEMENT

GARAGE
21'-0" x 23'-0"

BONUS ROOM ABOVE

◄ 69'-4' ►

62'-9"

Plan #F01-101012

Dimensions: 69'4" W x 62'9" D

Levels: 1

Heated Square Footage: 2,288

Bedrooms: 3

Bathrooms: 2½

Foundation: Crawl space, slab or walkout

Materials List Available: No

Price Category: H

Images provided by designer/architect.

CAD FILE AVAILABLE

Living Room

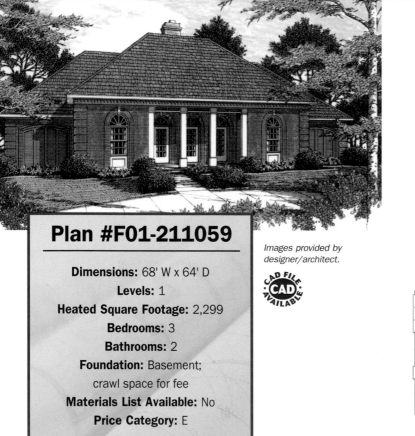

Plan #F01-211059

Dimensions: 68' W x 64' D

Levels: 1

Heated Square Footage: 2,299

Bedrooms: 3

Bathrooms: 2

Foundation: Basement; crawl space for fee

Materials List Available: No

Price Category: E

Images provided by designer/architect.

CAD FILE AVAILABLE

Bonus Area

bonus rm
21 x 16

dn

garage
22 x 22

sto 18 x 6

Copyright by designer/architect.

porch 20 x 8

dinette

study / home off
16 x 13

sun rm
16 x 10

living
20 x 20

kit

fireplace

built-in entertainment ctr

pan

br 3
12 x 12

br 2
12 x 12

foy

dining
13 x 12

mbr
22 x 13

porch 20 x 6

Plan #F01-321371

Dimensions: 68' W x 58'5" D

Levels: 1

Heated Square Footage: 2,305

Bedrooms: 4

Bathrooms: 2½

Foundation: Crawl space, slab or basement

Materials List Available: Yes

Price Category: E

Images provided by designer/architect.

CAD FILE AVAILABLE

Plan #F01-111017

Dimensions: 61' W x 70' D

Levels: 1

Heated Square Footage: 2,323

Bedrooms: 3

Bathrooms: 2½

Foundation: Slab or crawl space

Materials List Available: No

Price Category: F

Images provided by designer/architect.

Copyright by designer/architect.

storage
22' x 6'

garage
22' x 22'

Copyright by designer/architect.

disp. stairs

utility
13' x 9'

eating
12' x 12'

porch
20' x 8'

office/nursery
17' x 8'

books

kit
14' x 11'

living
20' x 20'
sloped clg.

sunroom
16' x 10'

wic.
10' x 8'

shr

ref.

pan
china

12' clg. in this area

bath

wic.
7' x 6'

mbr
24' x 13'

dining
13' x 12'
12' clg

foy
10'x5'

wet bar

clo.

br 3
12' x 12'

bath
10' x 11'

br 2
14' x 12'

sitting
area

porch 20' x 6'

Plan #F01-211151

Images provided by designer/architect.

Dimensions: 68' W x 72' D

Levels: 1

Heated Square Footage: 2,328

Bedrooms: 3

Bathrooms: 2

Foundation: Crawl space; basement for fee

Materials List Available: No

Price Category: E

Copyright by designer/architect.

11'-1" HIGH
STEPPED CLG
MSTR BEDRM
13'-0"x 19'-0"

COV. PORCH

FR GL DR

MSTR
BATH

WICL   WICL

BUILT-IN

10'-7" HIGH
STEPPED CLG
GREAT RM
17'-4" x 20'-8"

BKFST RM
10'-0"x
15'-0"

BEDRM #2
14'-4"x 11'-0"

BATH

KITCHEN
14'-0"x 14'-2"

BEDRM #3
11'-0"x
13'-0"

FOY

DINING RM
11'-0"x
15'-0"

TWO CAR GARAGE
20'-0"x 20'-6"

VAULTED
BEDRM #4
12'-0"x
13'-0"

PORCH

ALT LOCATION OF GAR DRS.

UNFIN. ATTIC
49'-10" x 17'-0"

UPPER CEILING
OF GREAT RM

DN

OPTIONAL LOFT AREA
WITH OPT. RAILING
OVERLOOKING GREAT ROOM

Bonus Area

Plan #F01-131045

Images provided by designer/architect.

Dimensions: 81'4" W x 68'3" D

Levels: 1

Heated Square Footage: 2,347

Bedrooms: 4

Bathrooms: 2½

Foundation: Crawl space or slab; basement for fee

Materials List Available: Yes

Price Category: F

1,501–2,500 sq. ft.

Plan #F01-191027

Dimensions: 62' W x 42' D

Levels: 1

Heated Square Footage: 2,354

Bedrooms: 4

Bathrooms: 2½

Foundation: Crawl space or slab

Materials List Available: No

Price Category: F

Images provided by designer/architect.

COVERED PORCH 2
11'-10" X 6'-0"

GREAT ROOM
20'-0" X 24'-0"

BEDROOM 2
13'-10" X 13'-0"

CLOSET
8'-0" X 10'-0"

LAUNDRY
8'-0" X 10'-0"

BREAKFAST AREA
12'-0" X 9'-9"

M. BATH

KITCHEN
12'-0" X 14'-3"

1/2 B

BATH 2

CLO.

CLO.

MASTER BEDROOM
16'-0" X 16'-0"

DINING ROOM
12'-0" X 12'-0"

FOYER

HALL

STUDY OR
BEDROOM 4
13'-0" X 13'-0"

BEDROOM 3
13'-10" X 13'-0"

COVERED PORCH 1
62'-0" X 7'-0"

Plan #F01-761031

Dimensions: 76'4" W x 52' D

Levels: 1

Heated Square Footage: 2,156

Bedrooms: 3

Bathrooms: 2

Foundation: Basement

Materials List Available: Yes

Price Category: D

Images provided by designer/architect.

CAD FILE AVAILABLE

MBr
15-5x17-4
Vaulted
Opt Coffer

Porch

Great Rm
17-10x20-7
Vaulted

Porch

Br 2
12-11x10-5

Kitchen
11-9x12-7

Brkfst
10-9x12-7

Laun/
Mud Rm

Dining Rm
12-8x12-5
13' Tray Clg

Foyer

Br 3
12-11x10-9

Garage
23-4x23-4

Porch

Plan #F01-241001

Dimensions: 65' W x 56'3" D

Levels: 1

Heated Square Footage: 2,350

Bedrooms: 3

Bathrooms: 2½

Foundation: Slab

Materials List Available: No

Price Category: E

Images provided by designer/architect.

Classic, traditional rooflines combine with arched windows to draw immediate attention to this lovely three-bedroom home.

Features:

- Great Room: The foyer introduces you to this impressive great room, with its grand 10-ft. ceiling and handsome fireplace.

- Kitchen: Certain to become the hub of such a family-oriented home, this spacious kitchen, which adjoins the breakfast area and a delightful sunroom, features an abundance of counter space, a pantry, and a convenient eating bar.

- Master Suite: You will enjoy the privacy and comfort of this master suite, which features a whirlpool tub, split vanities, and a separate shower.

- Study: Adjourn to the front of the house and enjoy the quiet confines of this private study with built-in bookshelves to work, read, or just relax.

SMARTtip

Kitchen Counters

Make use of counter inserts to help with the cooking chores. For example, ceramic tiles inlaid in a laminate counter create a heat-proof landing zone near the range. A marble or granite insert is tailor-made for pastry chefs. And a butcher-block inlay is a great addition to the food prep area.

Images provided by designer/architect.

Plan #F01-131052

Dimensions: 67' W x 63'10" D

Levels: 1

Heated Square Footage: 2,367

Bedrooms: 2

Bathrooms: 2

Foundation: Crawl space or slab; basement for fee

Materials List Available: Yes

Price Category: E

The front and back turrets, in combination with the vaulted ceilings and unusually shaped rooms, make this house a treasure.

Features:

- Covered Porch: The circular covered front porch is an endlessly versatile area.

- Dining Room: The shape of this room echoes that of the front porch. Windows let in plenty of light; the ceiling is vaulted; and columns separate the room from the great room.

- Great Room: A fireplace, door to the patio, and vaulted ceiling highlight this room.

- Library: Use this room, with its deep bay, as a bedroom, or turn it into a den or media room.

- Kitchen: The unique styled center island and U-shaped counter make this a convenient work space for the chef of this home.

- Master Suite: You'll love the turreted sitting room, tray ceiling, two walk-in closets, whirlpool tub, separate shower, and a double vanity.

Rear View

Copyright by designer/architect.

Plan #F01-211009

Dimensions: 72' W x 60' D

Levels: 1

Heated Square Footage: 2,396

Bedrooms: 4

Bathrooms: 2

Foundation: Slab; crawl space for fee

Materials List Available: Yes

Price Category: E

Beautiful arched windows lend a luxurious feeling to the exterior of this one-story home.

Features:

- Ceiling Height: 9 ft. unless otherwise noted.

- Entry: Guests will be greeted by a dramatic 12-ft. ceiling in this elegant foyer.

- Living Room: The 12-ft. ceiling continues through the foyer into this inviting living room. Everyone will feel welcomed by the crackling fire in the handsome fireplace.

- Covered Porch: When the weather is warm, invite guests to step out of the living room directly into this covered porch.

- Kitchen: This bright and cheery kitchen is designed for the way we live today. It includes a pantry and an angled eating bar that will see plenty of impromptu family meals.

- Energy-Efficient Walls: The exterior walls of this home are framed with 2x6 lumber instead of 2x4. The extra thickness makes room for more insulation to lower your heating and cooling bills.

Images provided by designer/architect.

Copyright by designer/architect.

SMARTtip

Ornaments in a Garden

Placement is everything with ornaments in a garden. Some elements are best sitting by themselves. Others are better when they are part of a cohesive whole, perhaps placed in the greenery at a corner or flanking a structure.

Plan #F01-321037

Dimensions: 78'8" W x 50'6" D
Levels: 1
Heated Square Footage: 2,397
Bedrooms: 3
Bathrooms: 2
Foundation: Walkout basement
Materials List Available: Yes
Price Category: F

Images provided by designer/architect.

Come home to this three-bedroom stucco home with arched windows.

Features:

- **Dining Room:** Just off of the entry is this formal room, with its vaulted ceiling and handy access to serving directly from the kitchen.

- **Great Room:** This large room has a vaulted ceiling and a fireplace. The focal point of this room is the large wall of windows and descending stairs to the atrium.

- **Kitchen:** A large pantry and an abundance of counter space make this kitchen a functional work space. The corner pantry allows for plenty of extra storage space.

- **Master Suite:** This suite has a double-door entry, an impressive bay window, and a large walk-in closet. The private bath comes complete with separate vanities, a step-up corner tub, a shower, and a private toilet closet.

- **Bedrooms:** The two additional bedrooms share a common bathroom.

Images provided by designer/architect.

Plan #F01-561005

Dimensions: 58'4" W x 72' D
Levels: 1
Heated Square Footage: 2,358
Bedrooms: 3
Bathrooms: 2
Foundation: Basement
Materials List Available: No
Price Category: E

CAD FILE AVAILABLE

This magnificent home design, with its traditional front porch and rear screened-in porch, is more than just a home.

Features:

- Great Room: Gather by the glowing fire on cold nights, or expand your entertaining space any other time. This great room is at the center of everything and has plenty of space for friends, family, and anyone else you can think to invite.

- Kitchen: A built-in pantry and ample counter space make a great work area for the family cook. An open transition to the breakfast area simplifies morning chaos, while a defined separation formalizes the dining room.

- Master Suite: This area is a welcome retreat where you can shut out the frenzied world and simply relax. The attached master bath includes dual walk-in closets, two sinks, a standing shower, and a separate tub — perfect for busy mornings and romantic evenings.

- Secondary Bedrooms: These bedrooms boast ample closet space and equal distance to a full bathroom.

Rear Elevation

Copyright by designer/architect.

Plan #F01-151002

Dimensions: 67' W x 66' D
Levels: 1
Heated Square Footage: 2,444
Bedrooms: 3
Bathrooms: 2½
Foundation: Crawl space or slab; basement or walkout for fee
Materials List Available: No
Price Category: J

CAD FILE AVAILABLE

This gracious, traditional home is designed for practicality and convenience.

Features:

- Ceiling Height: 9-ft. except as noted below.

- Great Room: This room is ideal for entertaining, thanks to its lovely fireplace and French doors that open to the covered rear porch. Built-in cabinets give convenient storage space.

- Family Room: With access to the kitchen as well as the rear porch, this room will become your family's "headquarters."

- Study: Enjoy the quiet in this room with its 12-ft. ceiling and doorway to a private patio on the side of the house.

- Dining Room: Take advantage of the 8-in. wood columns and 12-ft. ceilings to create a formal dining area.

- Kitchen: An eat-in bar is a great place to snack, and the handy computer nook allows the kids to do their homework while you cook.

- Breakfast Room: Opening from the kitchen, this area gives added space for the family to gather any time.

- Master Suite: Featuring a 10-ft. boxed ceiling, the master bedroom also has a door way that opens onto the covered rear porch. The master bathroom has a step-up whirlpool tub, separate shower, and twin vanities with a makeup area.

Copyright by designer/architect.

Plan #F01-661004

Dimensions: 60'6" W x 71'8" D

Levels: 1

Heated Square Footage: 2,397

Bedrooms: 3

Bathrooms: 2½

Foundation: Slab

Materials List Available: No

Price Category: E

Images provided by designer/architect.

CAD FILE AVAILABLE

Front View

Plan #F01-271074

Dimensions: 68' W x 86' D

Levels: 1

Heated Square Footage: 2,400

Bedrooms: 4

Bathrooms: 3

Foundation: Crawl space, slab, or basement

Materials List Available: No

Price Category: E

Images provided by designer/architect.

CAD FILE AVAILABLE

Plan #F01-761006

Dimensions: 42'4" W x 54' D

Levels: 1

Heated Square Footage: 1,582

Bedrooms: 3

Bathrooms: 2

Foundation: Basement

Materials List Available: Yes

Price Category: C

Images provided by designer/architect.

CAD FILE AVAILABLE

Kitchen View

Copyright by designer/architect.

Plan #F01-151852

Dimensions: 70'2" W x 86'8" D

Levels: 1

Heated Square Footage: 2,424

Bedrooms: 4

Bathrooms: 3

Foundation: Crawl space or slab; basement or walkout for fee

Materials List Available: Yes

Price Category: H

Images provided by designer/architect.

CAD FILE AVAILABLE

Bonus Area

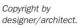

PLAYROOM
16'-10" X 14'-3"

Plan #F01-241017

Dimensions: 74'4" W x 55'4" D

Levels: 1

Heated Square Footage: 2,431

Bedrooms: 4

Bathrooms: 2½

Foundation: Slab; crawl space for fee

Materials List Available: No

Price Category: E

Images provided by designer/architect.

Copyright by designer/architect.

Bonus Area

Copyright by designer/architect.

Plan #F01-351203

Dimensions: 73'6" W x 62' D

Levels: 1

Heated Square Footage: 2,447

Bedrooms: 4

Bathrooms: 2½

Foundation: Crawl space or basement

Materials List Available: Yes

Price Category: H

Images provided by designer/architect.

CAD FILE
CAD
AVAILABLE

Plan #F01-321019

Dimensions: 70'8" W x 70' D
Levels: 1
Heated Square Footage: 2,452
Bedrooms: 4
Bathrooms: 2½
Foundation: Basement
Materials List Available: Yes
Price Category: E

Images provided by designer/architect.

CAD FILE AVAILABLE — CAD

Plan #F01-121053

Dimensions: 66' W x 68' D
Levels: 1
Heated Square Footage: 2,456
Bedrooms: 3
Bathrooms: 2½
Foundation: Basement
Materials List Available: Yes
Price Category: E

Images provided by designer/architect.

SMARTtip

Installing Plastic Molding

Foam trim is best cut with a backsaw. Power miter saws with fine-toothed blades also work. Larger-toothed blades tend to tear the foam unevenly.

Plan #F01-161037

Dimensions: 46' W x 59'4" D

Levels: 1

Heated Square Footage: 2,469

Main Level Sq. Ft.: 1,462

Basement Level Sq. Ft.: 1,007

Bedrooms: 2

Bathrooms: 2½

Foundation: Walkout; basement for fee

Materials List Available: Yes

Price Category: E

Images provided by designer/architect.

Main Level

Optional Screened Porch 12 x 12

Deck

Dining 13' x 15'4"

Great Room 15' x 18'6"

Master Bedroom 16'4" X 14'

Kitchen 13' x 12'6"

Foyer

Dress.

Bath

Laun.

walk-in closet

Porch

Garage 22'2" x 26'5"

Copyright by designer/architect.

Basement Level

Library 12'7" X 12'

Bath

Hall

Rec Room 22'6" X 18'7"

Bedroom 14'5" X 14'10"

Wet Bar

UP

Basement

Unexcavated

Unexcavated

Rear Elevation

Plan #F01-351088

Dimensions: 66'8" W x 73'2" D

Levels: 1

Heated Square Footage: 2,500

Bedrooms: 4

Bathrooms: 3

Foundation: Crawl space, basement or slab

Materials List Available: Yes

Price Category: H

Images provided by designer/architect.

CAD FILE AVAILABLE

Copyright by designer/architect.

Bonus Area

Closet 6-1 x 6-6

Master Bath 14-4 x 13-10

Master Bedroom 14-6 x 15-6 (Trayed) 10-0 Clg. Ht. 9-0 Clg. Ht.

Closet 8-2 x 8-2

Bedroom 3 12-0 x 12-0 9-0 Clg. Ht.

Covered Porch 18-0 x 7-6

Keeping / Breakfast 12-0 x 17-4 9-0 Clg. Ht.

Office / Nursery 7-6 x 7-8

Bedroom 4 11-2 x 11-10 9-0 Clg. Ht.

Hall 1

Great Room 17-8 x 17-0 (Clear) VAULT.

Hall 3

Bath 2 8-0 x 7-7

Bath 3 8-10 x 5-0

Laun. 7-2 x 9-2

Kitchen 12-0 x 12-8

Stor.

Bedroom 2 12-0 x 12-0 9-0 Clg. Ht.

Foyer 5-8 x 12-10

Dining 12-0 x 12-6 10-0 Clg. Ht.

Covered Porch 31-0 x 6-0

Two Car Garage 23-0 x 22-2

Unfinished Bonus Room 13-0 x 22-2 8-0 Clg. Ht.

Outline of Floor Below

Images provided by designer/architect.

Copyright by designer/architect.

Plan #F01-161196

Dimensions: 59' W x 59'6" D

Levels: 1

Heated Square Footage: 2,469

Bedrooms: 3

Bathrooms: 2

Foundation: Basement or walkout; crawl space or slab for fee

Materials List Available: Yes

Price Category: E

Images provided by designer/architect.

Copyright by designer/architect.

Plan #F01-121003

Dimensions: 76' W x 55'4" D

Levels: 1

Heated Square Footage: 2,498

Bedrooms: 4

Bathrooms: 2½

Foundation: Basement; crawl space or slab for fee

Materials List Available: Yes

Price Category: E

Porches and Three-Season Rooms

At its simplest, a three-season room or sunroom is a porch modified to keep the weather out. A three-season room protects you from wind, rain, and snow, but it isn't heated or cooled. A sunroom not only keeps the elements out, it offers a heated and cooled environment similar to any other room in your house. If you're looking for a protected spot to get some fresh air, and you don't mind what temperature that air is, consider a three-season room.

If you're a sun lover who'd rather not brave freezing cold or oppressive heat to bask in the sunlight, think about a sunroom. In this article we'll look at what goes into creating each of these rooms.

Traditional-style sunrooms, opposite, are often made with standard windows rather than floor-to-ceiling glass.

This manufactured addition could be either a three-season room or a sunroom, depending on the type of glass chosen.

Room Options

You can convert an existing porch to a three-season room by installing glass and screen panels and a storm door between posts or columns. Or you can build a new three-season addition with floor-to-ceiling window-and-screen panels.

Because it is uninsulated and unheated, a three-season room won't get much winter use in cold climates. But on those late fall or early spring days when a porch would be uncomfortably chilly, a three-season room can warm up nicely as radiant heat from the sun is captured in the enclosed space. Where winters are warm, the off season may be the summer, when the uninsulated, unairconditioned space may get too toasty.

Sunrooms are by definition habitable in all seasons, though the demands of insulation, heating, and cooling make them more expensive than three-season rooms. They may be conversions of porches, patios, or decks. They can be custom-

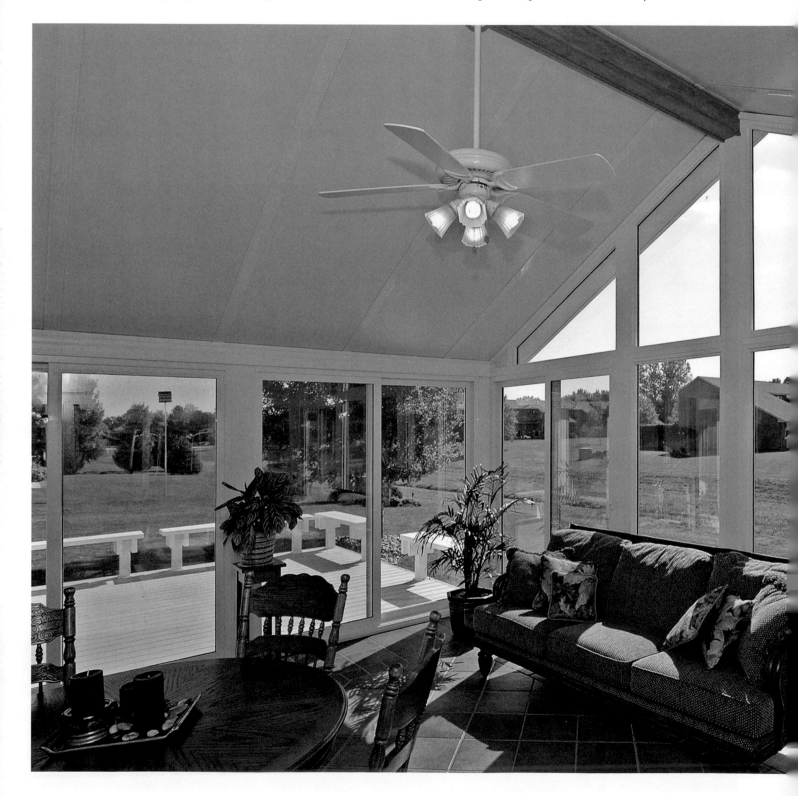

made from the ground up. Or they can be manufactured and installed in a matter of days.

Many sunrooms are highly finished and indistinguishable in style, detail, and furnishings from other rooms in the house. Or they may have a distinctive style all their own.

Whether they are conversions, custom built, or factory made, three-season rooms and sunrooms have many similarities. Their basic structures are often the same. Replace single-pane glass with insulated glass and add insulation to the walls,

floors, and roof, and add a source of heating and cooling, and a three-season room becomes a sunroom.

Porch Conversions

Many open-air porches can be converted to three-season rooms. How easily this can be done depends a great deal on how ornate the porch is. It's relatively simple to install window and screen units and a door on a porch that has rectilinear posts and simple railings. Adding windows and a door to a

A manufactured room was cleverly adapted to convert this porch to a three-season room, above and below.

Framing a Porch for Windows

If an opening on a porch is already rectangular and is plumb and level, you can size a custom-built window and frame to fit in that opening, attaching it to the posts, deck or railing, and top beam. Or you can frame new openings to fit standard-size manufactured windows or custom windows of a size you desire. Windows for porch conversions are often housed in wood frames because a carpenter can often make them on site. You can also have aluminum frames custom-built with individual windows and screens made to fit.

If porch openings are irregularly shaped, it's usually more cost-effective to modify the openings than to build oddly shaped windows. This is especially true for windows with moving parts, such as sashes or louvers. Porches with round or molded columns, sloped floors, or elaborate brackets can be framed to accept rectilinear windows, as shown in the drawings at night. Porch decks usually slope away from the house. Openings for windows added along the slope are best framed to create a level bottom because rectilinear windows are much cheaper than trapezoidal ones. Also, glass that rests less than 18 inches above the deck is required by code to be tempered, which will increase the cost. You can frame the opening higher to accommodate standard glass.

Simple Framing for Porch Windows

Header

Wood Frame

Post

Fix custom-built woodscreens and storms or aluminum combination windows in frame

Window or Solid Panel

Fit frame around existing post moldings

Scribed Framing for Porch Windows

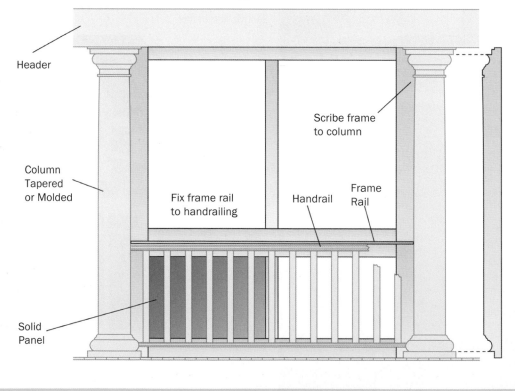

Header

Column Tapered or Molded

Solid Panel

Fix frame rail to handrailing

Handrail

Frame Rail

Scribe frame to column

A window frame has been carefully scribed to the Ionic capital and base and the gentle curve of the column shaft in the conversion shown above.

porch that has tapered or heavily molded columns, elaborate brackets, and complex or curved railings requires more thought, more construction skills, and usually more money. (See "Framing a Porch for Windows," left.)

Door, window, and screen units are often much the same for simple and complicated installations alike. The extra cost and installation finesse comes from figuring out how to fill in between rectangular door, window, and screen units and the existing curved and filigreed porch columns and railings.

Converting a porch to a sunroom is a bit more difficult and expensive. Insulated windows and doors are more costly than those with single-pane glass. Insulating an existing porch floor and roof isn't necessarily expensive or difficult, but it may not be terribly effective, either. Nevertheless, charming sunrooms have been made from porches.

Before you consider how to convert an existing porch, make sure it is structurally sound. Check for good footings and foundations; no rotting or deteriorating posts, joists, floor boards, or roof members; and no leaning or tilting. If it's going to cost a lot of money to fix the structure before you convert the space, you should probably tear off the existing porch and build from scratch.

Converting a Deck

A deck is often an ideal site for a three-season room or sunroom addition. Decks are usually located where sun, shade, and wind conditions on your property are optimal. They are usually adjacent to a room in the house that is desirable for connection to a three-season room or sunroom. They may already have a door or sliding door suitable for access to the new room. And they can provide, at the least, a ready-made floor or subfloor.

Before you convert a deck, you'll need to check its footings to see if they are large enough to carry the additional load of walls and roof. A contractor or codes department can help you with the calculations. If the footings are insufficient, you may be able to enlarge them with additional concrete. Or you may need to build temporary supports, tear out the existing footings, and re-pour.

Straight columns are relatively easy to fill in to enclose a porch, right. Turned columns and a railing, far right, make enclosing a porch a more complicated project.

Traditional wooden storm windows and screens enclose this three-season porch conversion, below.

Embedded in the wall, the original porch columns are a striking feature of this converted sunroom, opposite.

Images provided by designer/architect.

Plan #F01-151188

Dimensions: 63'4" W x 59'10" D
Levels: 1
Heated Square Footage: 2,525
Bedrooms: 3
Bathrooms: 2½
Foundation: Crawl space or slab; basement or walkout for fee
Materials List Available: No
Price Category: I

This Southwestern-inspired home has a beautiful layout that you will love.

Features:

- Great Room: Opening out from the gallery, this great room is truly at the heart of this home. Built-in shelves and a media center flank a fireplace for a lovely setting.

- Kitchen: This kitchen features plenty of counter space for all of your needs. A center island provides additional space for prepping meals or holding dishes.

- Master Suite: Unwind in this wonderful master suite, complete with a whirlpool tub, a glass shower, separate vanities, and a spacious walk-in closet.

- Secondary Bedrooms: Located near the master suite, two secondary bedrooms are perfect for siblings. A shared bath features a private toilet and bath area.

Plan #F01-241008

Dimensions: 65' W x 56'8" D
Levels: 1
Heated Square Footage: 2,526
Bedrooms: 4
Bathrooms: 3
Foundation: Crawl space, slab, or basement
Materials List Available: No
Price Category: E

A covered back porch — with access from the master suite and the breakfast area — makes this traditional home ideal for a setting near a golf course or with a backyard pool.

Features:

- Great Room: From the foyer, guests enter this spacious and comfortable great room, which features a handsome fireplace.

- Kitchen: This kitchen — the hub of this family-oriented home — is a joy in which to work, thanks to abundant counter space, a pantry, a convenient eating bar, and an adjoining breakfast area and sunroom.

- Master Suite: Enjoy the quiet comfort of this coffered-ceiling master suite, which features a dual vanity and separate walk-in closets.

- Additional Bedrooms: Two secondary bedrooms, which share a full bath, are located at the opposite end of the house from the master suite. Bedroom 4 — in front of the house — can be converted into a study.

Images provided by designer/architect.

Optional Bonus Area

Copyright by designer/architect.

SMARTtip

Traditional-Style Kitchen Cabinetry

You can modify stock kitchen cabinetry to enjoy fine furniture-quality details. Prefabricated trims may be purchased at local lumber mills and home centers. For example, crown molding, applied to the top of stock cabinetry and stained or painted to match the door style, may be all you need. Likewise, you can replace hardware with reproduction polished-brass door and drawer knobs or pulls for a finishing touch.

Plan #F01-151383

Dimensions: 70'4" W x 57'2" D

Levels: 1

Heated Square Footage: 2,534

Bedrooms: 3

Bathrooms: 2

Foundation: Crawl space or slab; basement or walkout for fee

Materials List Available: No

Price Category: K

Images provided by designer/architect.
This home, as shown in the photograph, may differ from the actual blueprints.
For more information, please check the floor plans carefully.

The arched entry of the covered porch welcomes you into this magnificent home.

Features:

- Foyer: Welcome your guests into this warm foyer before leading them into the impressive dining room with magnificent columns framing the entry.

- Great Room: After dinner, your guests will enjoy conversation in this spacious room, complete with a fireplace and built-ins.

- Study: Beautiful French doors open into this quiet space, where you'll be able to concentrate on that work away from the office.

- Rear Porch: This relaxing spot may be reached from the breakfast room or your secluded master suite.

Copyright by designer/architect.

Front View

Plan #F01-271081

Dimensions: 86' W x 54' D

Levels: 1

Heated Square Footage: 2,539

Bedrooms: 3

Bathrooms: 2

Foundation: Slab

Materials List Available: No

Price Category: E

Images provided by designer/architect.

This traditional home is sure to impress your guests and even your neighbors.

Features:

- **Living Room:** This quiet space off of the foyer is perfect for pleasant conversation.

- **Family Room:** A perfect gathering spot, this room is nicely enhanced by a fireplace.

- **Kitchen:** This room easily serves the bayed morning room and the formal dining room.

- **Master Suite:** The master bedroom overlooks a side patio, and boasts a private bath with a skylight and a whirlpool tub.

- **Library:** This cozy room is perfect for curling up with a good novel. It would also make a great extra bedroom.

Copyright by designer/architect.

SMARTtip

Determining Curtain Length

Follow length guidelines for foolproof results, but remember that they're not rules. Go ahead and play with curtain and drapery lengths. Instead of shortening long panels at the hem, for instance, take up excess material by blousing them over tiebacks for a pleasing effect.

Plan #F01-151140

Dimensions: 67'2" W x 55'10" D

Levels: 1

Heated Square Footage: 2,525

Bedrooms: 4

Bathrooms: 3

Foundation: Crawl space or slab; basement or walkout for fee

Materials List Available: No

Price Category: I

Images provided by designer/architect.

Copyright by designer/architect.

Great Room

Kitchen

Plan #F01-191058

Dimensions: 80' W x 56' D

Levels: 1

Heated Square Footage: 2,550

Bedrooms: 5

Bathrooms: 3

Foundation: Slab

Materials List Available: No

Price Category: E

Images provided by designer/architect.

Copyright by designer/architect.

Kitchen

Rear View

Copyright by designer/architect.

Patio · Brkfst 12-3x10-0 · Great Rm 17-7x20-1 11' Clg · MBr 14-9x16-8 Coffer Clg · Br 2 11-5x11-4 · Kitchen 12-3x10-5 · Dining 11-6x11-1 10'-6" Tray Clg · Foyer 11' Clg · Study 11-5x11-1 · Br 3 11-5x11-1 · Laun/ Mud Rm · Porch Barrel Vault · Opt. Attic Space · Garage 22-10x24-8

Plan #F01-761019

Images provided by designer/architect.

CAD FILE AVAILABLE

Dimensions: 73' W x 75'4" D
Levels: 1
Heated Square Footage: 2,814
Bedrooms: 3
Bathrooms: 3½
Foundation: Basement
Materials List Available: Yes
Price Category: F

Copyright by designer/architect.

GARAGE 26'-4" X 32'-2" · ATTIC STORAGE · BRKFST. ROOM 14'-5" X 10'-2" · GRILLING PORCH 18'-2" X 6'-8" · MASTER SUITE 16'-0" X 13'-0" · 42" HIGH BAR · KITCHEN 14'-5" X 10'-0" · GREAT ROOM 18'-2" X 19'-6" · M.BATH · W.I.C. 12'-6" X 6'-0" · STOR. · BENCH KID'S NOOK · BUILT-INS · BATH · BEDROOM 2 13'-2" X 12'-0" · PANTRY · LAU. 8'-5" X 9'-6" · DINING ROOM 12'-2" X 12'-2" · FOYER 7'-8" X 11'-10" · OFFICE / GUEST ROOM 11'-10" X 12'-2" · BEDROOM 3 14'-0" X 12'-8" · COVERED PORCH 33'-6" X 8'-0"

Plan #F01-151486

Images provided by designer/architect.

CAD FILE AVAILABLE

Dimensions: 74'7" W x 70'6" D
Levels: 1
Heated Square Footage: 2,556
Bedrooms: 4
Bathrooms: 3
Foundation: Crawl space or slab; basement for fee
Materials List Available: No
Price Category: I

2,501–3,000 sq. ft.

Main Level

Alternate Floor Plan

Copyright by designer/architect.

Images provided by designer/architect.

Plan #F01-421009

Dimensions: 64'9" W x 59' D

Levels: 1

Heated Square Footage: 2,649

Bedrooms: 3

Bathrooms: 2

Foundation: Crawl space, slab, or basement

Materials List Available: Yes

Price Category: F

Copyright by designer/architect.

Images provided by designer/architect.

Plan #F01-661007

Dimensions: 66'4" W x 74'4" D

Levels: 1

Heated Square Footage: 2,660

Bedrooms: 4

Bathrooms: 3

Foundation: Slab

Materials List Available: No

Price Category: F

Plan #F01-191028

Dimensions: 80' W x 63' D
Levels: 1
Heated Square Footage: 2,669
Bedrooms: 4
Bathrooms: 3½
Foundation: Slab, crawl space or basement
Materials List Available: No
Price Category: H

Images provided by designer/architect.

Plan #F01-151802

Dimensions: 75'2" W x 57'4" D
Levels: 1
Heated Square Footage: 2,675
Bedrooms: 3
Bathrooms: 2
Foundation: Crawl space or slab
Materials List Available: No
Price Category: I

Images provided by designer/architect.

Plan #F01-101013

Dimensions: 72' W x 66' D
Levels: 1
Heated Square Footage: 2,564
Bedrooms: 3
Bathrooms: 2½
Foundation: Walkout; crawl space, slab or basement for fee
Materials List Available: Yes
Price Category: H

CAD FILE AVAILABLE

This exciting design combines a striking classic exterior with a highly functional floor plan.

Features:

- Ceiling Height: 9 ft. unless otherwise noted.

- Family Room: This warm and inviting room measures 18 ft. x 22 ft. It features a 14-ft. ceiling and a rear wall of windows. French doors lead to an enormous deck.

- Kitchen: This unique angled kitchen is open to the hearth room and eating areas, all of which enjoy vaulted ceilings and are surrounded by windows. The hearth room has a TV niche.

- Master Suite: This 19-ft. x 18-ft. master suite is truly sumptuous, with its 12-ft. ceiling, sitting area, two walk-in closets, and full-featured bath.

- Secondary Bedrooms: Each of the secondary bedrooms measures 11 ft. x 14 ft. and has direct access to a shared bath.

- Bonus Room: Just beyond the entry are stairs leading to this bonus room, which measures approximately 12 ft. x 21 ft. — plenty of room for storage or future expansion.

Master Bedroom

Plan #F01-441009

Dimensions: 94' W x 53' D
Levels: 1
Heated Square Footage: 2,650
Bedrooms: 4
Bathrooms: 2½
Foundation: Crawl space; slab or basement available for fee
Materials List Available: Yes
Price Category: G

You'll love to call this plan home. It's large enough for the whole family and has a facade that will make you the envy of the area.

Features:

- Foyer: The covered porch protects the entry, which has a transom and sidelights to brighten this space.

- Great Room: To the left of the foyer, beyond decorative columns, lies this vaulted room, with its fireplace and media center. Additional columns separate the room from the vaulted formal dining room.

- Kitchen: A casual nook and this island work center are just around the corner from the great room. The second covered porch can be reached via a door in the nook.

- Master Suite: This luxurious space boasts a vaulted salon, a private niche that could be a small study, and a view of the front yard. The master bath features a spa tub, separate shower, compartmented toilet, huge walk-in closet, and access to the laundry room.

- Bedrooms: The two additional bedrooms are located at the back of the plan and share the Jack-and-Jill bathroom.

Copyright by designer/architect.

Rear Elevation

Images provided by designer/architect.

Plan #F01-121163

Dimensions: 65'10" W x 75'6" D
Levels: 1
Heated Square Footage: 2,679
Bedrooms: 4
Bathrooms: 3
Foundation: Slab; basement for fee
Materials List Available: Yes
Price Category: F

Large rooms give this home a spacious feel in a modest footprint.

Features:

- **Family Room:** This area is the central gathering place in the home. The windows to the rear fill the area with natural light and overlook the porch. The fireplace takes the chill off on cool winter nights.

- **Kitchen:** This peninsula kitchen with raised bar is open into the family room and the breakfast area. The built-in pantry is a welcomed storage area for today's family.

- **Master Suite:** This secluded area features large windows with a view of the backyard. The master bath boasts a large walk-in closet, his and her vanities and a compartmentalized lavatory area.

- **Secondary Bedrooms:** Bedroom 2 has its own access to the main bathroom, while bedrooms 3 and 4 share a Jack-and-Jill bathroom. All bedrooms feature walk-in closets.

Copyright by designer/architect.

Images provided by designer/architect.

Plan #F01-211062

Dimensions: 74'6" W x 75' D
Levels: 1
Heated Square Footage: 2,682
Bedrooms: 4
Bathrooms: 3½
Foundation: Slab; crawl space for fee
Materials List Available: Yes
Price Category: F

If you're looking for a beautiful home that combines luxurious amenities with a separate, professional office space, this could be the one.

Features:

- **Living Room:** Enjoy an 11-ft. ceiling, brick fireplace, and built-in shelving in this room.

- **Dining Room:** A 2-story ceiling gives presence to this room.

- **Kitchen:** A breakfast bar here is open to the breakfast room beyond for ease of serving.

- **Breakfast Room:** A built-in corner china closet adds to the practicality you'll find here.

- **Office:** A separate entrance makes it possible to run a professional business from this home.

- **Master Suite:** Separated for privacy, this suite includes a double-bowl vanity and a walk-in closet.

- **Porch:** The rear screened porch opens to a courtyard where you'll love to entertain.

CAD FILE AVAILABLE

3 car garage 22 x 32

Copyright by designer/architect.

courtyard

wic

br 2 16 x 11

bath

screen porch 25 x 11

china

eating 11 x 10

bath

office 15 x 11

br 3 12 x 12

t.v.

wic

bath

family rm 21 x 17

11' clg

dw

kit 15x12

ref

pan

ct

ov

wic

shr

mbr 17 x 13

wic

br 4 12 x 12

living 19 x 14

11' clg

dining 13 x 12

2 story clg

util 12x6

W

d

br

lin

porch 26 x 5

Plan #F01-321027

Dimensions: 72' W x 68' D

Levels: 1

Heated Square Footage: 2,758

Bedrooms: 4

Bathrooms: 2½

Foundation: Basement

Materials List Available: Yes

Price Category: F

This stone-and-wood-sided four-bedroom home has country charm.

Features:

- Dining Room: You'll find this room with its high ceiling just off of the entry.

- Great Room: This large gathering area has a vaulted ceiling with skylights and a corner fireplace.

- Kitchen: This large U-shaped kitchen has an abundance of cabinets and opens into the breakfast area with a vaulted ceiling.

- Master Suite: This private area features a vaulted ceiling, corner fireplace and a walk-in closet. The master bath has a double-bowl vanity and soaking tub.

- Bedrooms: Three additional bedrooms share a common bath.

Copyright by designer/architect.

Plan #F01-211011

Dimensions: 84' W x 54' D
Levels: 1
Heated Square Footage: 2,791
Bedrooms: 4
Bathrooms: 2
Foundation: Slab or crawl space;
basement for fee
Materials List Available: Yes
Price Category: F

Images provided by designer/architect.

CAD FILE AVAILABLE

Plenty of room plus an open, flexible floor plan make this a home that will adapt to your needs.

Features:

- Ceiling Height: 8 ft. unless otherwise noted.
- Living Room: This distinctive room features a 12-ft. ceiling and is designed so that it can also serve as a master suite with a sitting room or easily converted to anything that fits your family's needs.
- Family Room: The whole family will want to gather in this large, inviting family room.
- Morning Room: The family room blends into this sunny spot, which is perfect for informal family meals.
- Kitchen: This kitchen offers a smart layout. It is also contiguous to the family room.
- Master Suite: You'll look forward to the end of the day when you can enjoy this master suite. It includes a huge, luxurious master bath with two large walk-in closets and two vanity sinks.
- Optional Bedroom: This optional fourth bedroom is located so that it can easily serve as a library, den, office, or music room.

SMARTtip

Types of Decks

Ground-level decks resemble a low platform and are best for flat locations. They can be the most economical type to build because they don't require stairs.

Raised decks can rise just a few steps up or meet the second story of a house. Lifted high on post supports, they adapt well to uneven or sloped locations.

Multilevel decks feature two or more stories and are connected by stairways or ramps. They can follow the contours of a sloped lot, unifying the deck with the outdoors.

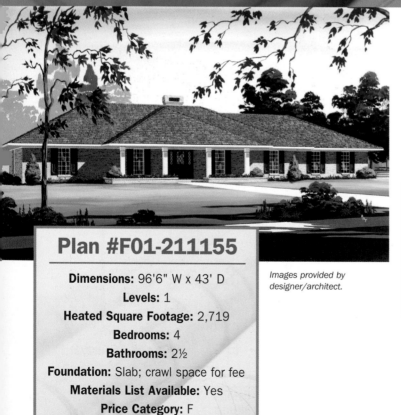

Plan #F01-321007

Dimensions: 76' W x 55'2" D
Levels: 1
Heated Square Footage: 2,695
Bedrooms: 3
Bathrooms: 2½
Foundation: Basement
Materials List Available: Yes
Price Category: G

Images provided by designer/architect.

Copyright by designer/architect.

SMARTtip

Decorative Poles

Drapery poles are supported by the brackets fastened to the window frame or wall. The brackets that are provided with the poles generally coordinate and blend in with the pole finish. Brackets can be simple but also decorative. If you opt for a spectacular, attention-grabbing bracket, consider choosing less showy finials for the ends of the pole.

Plan #F01-211155

Dimensions: 96'6" W x 43' D
Levels: 1
Heated Square Footage: 2,719
Bedrooms: 4
Bathrooms: 2½
Foundation: Slab; crawl space for fee
Materials List Available: Yes
Price Category: F

Images provided by designer/architect.

Copyright by designer/architect.

Bonus Area

BONUS ROOM
20'-0" X 14'-0"

Copyright by designer/architect.

Images provided by designer/architect.

CAD FILE AVAILABLE

Plan #F01-371095

Dimensions: 82'6" W x 62' D

Levels: 1

Heated Square Footage: 2,725

Bedrooms: 4

Bathrooms: 2½

Foundation: Crawl space, slab, or basement

Materials List Available: No

Price Category: F

Rear Elevation

Patio

Porch

Bedroom 15'9"x 13'1"

Breakfast 13'5"x 11'7"

Master Bedroom 14'5"x 18'7"

Bath

Kitchen 13'9"x14'

Living 20'x 19'3"

WIC

Dress

WIC

Bedroom 12'1"x 13'1"

Utility

Dining 12'7"x 16'1"

Foyer

Master Bath

Storage 12'1"x 6'3"

Porch

Bedroom 14'7"x 13'1"

Porch

Two-Car Garage 21'3"x 22'3"

Copyright by designer/architect.

Plan #F01-111018

Dimensions: 67' W x 79' D

Levels: 1

Heated Square Footage: 2,745

Bedrooms: 4

Bathrooms: 3½

Foundation: Slab or walkout

Materials List Available: No

Price Category: G

Images provided by designer/architect.

CAD FILE AVAILABLE

Plan #F01-151594

Dimensions: 65' W x 64'10" D

Levels: 1

Heated Square Footage: 2,760

Main Level Sq. Ft.: 2,406

Upper Level Sq. Ft.: 354

Bedrooms: 3

Bathrooms: 3½

Foundation: Crawl space or slab; basement or walkout for fee

Materials List Available: No

Price Category: I

Images provided by designer/architect.

Copyright by designer/architect.

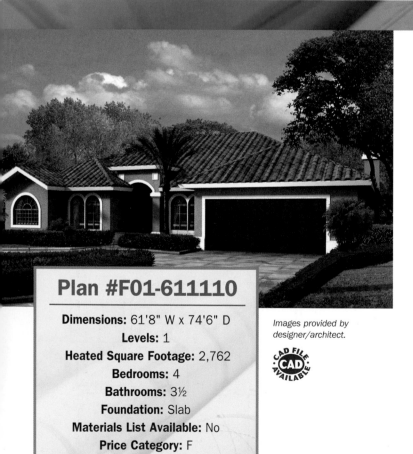

Plan #F01-611110

Dimensions: 61'8" W x 74'6" D

Levels: 1

Heated Square Footage: 2,762

Bedrooms: 4

Bathrooms: 3½

Foundation: Slab

Materials List Available: No

Price Category: F

Images provided by designer/architect.

Copyright by designer/architect.

Copyright by designer/architect.

Images provided by designer/architect.

Rear View

Plan #F01-161224

Dimensions: 87'4" W x 57'4" D

Levels: 1

Heated Square Footage: 2,796

Bedrooms: 2

Bathrooms: 2½

Foundation: Walkout

Materials List Available: Yes

Price Category: F

Plan #F01-111001

Dimensions: 66'8" W x 76'11" D

Levels: 1

Heated Square Footage: 2,832

Bedrooms: 4

Bathrooms: 2½

Foundation: Crawl space or slab

Materials List Available: No

Price Category: G

Images provided by designer/architect.

Images provided by designer/architect.

Plan #F01-181708

Dimensions: 53' W x 40' D

Levels: 1

Heated Square Footage: 2,800

Main Level Sq. Ft.: 1,400

Lower Level Sq. Ft.: 1,400

Bedrooms: 3

Bathrooms: 2

Foundation: Basement or walkout; crawl space or slab for fee

Materials List Available: Yes

Price Category: I

This gorgeous hillside home is designed for comfort and convenience.

Features:

- Great Room: No matter the time of day, this room will be filled with natural light from a sunlit wall of windows or a glowing fireplace.

- Dining Area: Not only does this dining room feature a beautiful bay of windows, but it also adjoins a deck where you might place a small table and chairs for picnic lunches with an elevated view.

- Kitchen: A unique element of this kitchen is the divided snack bar, which flanks the entry to the dining area and curves to provide more open space.

- Bedrooms: Each of these two nicely sized bedrooms has access to a bathroom. The front bedroom opens onto a small private deck.

Main Level

Lower Level

Images provided by designer/architect.

Plan #F01-151057

Dimensions: 73'6" W x 80'6" D
Levels: 1
Heated Square Footage: 2,951
Bedrooms: 4
Bathrooms: 3
Foundation: Crawl space or slab; basement or walkout for fee
Materials List Available: No
Price Category: K

The stucco exterior and large windows give this ranch an elegant look.

Features:

- Foyer: Enter the covered porch, and walk through the beautiful front door to this large foyer with entry closet.

- Entertaining: The large great room has a cozy fireplace and built-ins for casual get-togethers. The formal living room, also with a fireplace, is for special entertaining.

- Kitchen: This large U-shaped island kitchen has a raised bar and is open to the breakfast area and the great room. A short step though the door brings you onto the rear lanai.

- Master Suite: This private retreat has a fireplace and a sitting area with access to the rear lanai. The master bath features dual vanities, a whirlpool tub, a glass shower, and a separate toilet room.

 CAD FILE AVAILABLE

- Bedrooms: Three large bedrooms are located on the opposite side of the home to give the master suite privacy. Two bedrooms share a Jack and Jill bathroom. The third bedroom has access to a common bathroom.

Copyright by designer/architect.

Images provided by designer/architect.

Living Room

Plan #F01-111004

Dimensions: 76' W x 85' D

Levels: 1

Heated Square Footage: 2,968

Bedrooms: 4

Full Bathrooms: 3½

Foundation: Slab or crawl space

Materials List Available: No

Price Category: G

If you've been looking for a home that includes a special master suite, this one could be the answer to your dreams.

Features:

• Living Room: Make a sitting area around the fireplace here so that the whole family can enjoy the warmth on chilly days and winter evenings. A door from this room leads to the rear covered porch, making this room the heart of your home.

• Kitchen: An island with a cooktop makes cooking a pleasure in this well-designed kitchen, and the breakfast bar invites visitors at all times of day.

• Utility Room: A sink and a built-in ironing board make this room totally practical.

• Master Suite: A private fireplace in the corner sets a romantic tone for this bedroom, and the door to the covered porch allows you to sit outside on warm summer nights. The bath has two sinks, a divided walk-in closet, a standing shower, and a deluxe corner bathtub.

Bonus Area

Plan #F01-441010

Dimensions: 108'6" W x 59' D
Levels: 1
Heated Square Footage: 2,973
Bedrooms: 4
Bathrooms: 4½
Foundation: Crawl space;
slab or basement available for fee
Materials List Available: Yes
Price Category: G

Images provided by designer/architect.

Bordering on estate-sized, this plan borrows elements from Norman, Mediterranean, and English architecture.

Features:

• Great Room: This gathering area features a large bay window and a fireplace flanked with built-ins. The vaulted ceiling adds to the large feel of the area.

• Kitchen: This large island kitchen features a walk-in pantry and a built-in desk. The breakfast nook has access to the patio.

• Master Suite: This retreat features a vaulted ceiling in the sleeping area and access to the patio. The master bath boasts dual sinks, a stand-up shower, a spa tub, and a very large walk-in closet.

• Bedrooms: Two family bedrooms, each with its own private bathroom, have large closets.

Rear Elevation

Bonus Area

Main Level

NOOK
10/0 X 11/4
(9' CLG)

GREAT RM.
16/8 X 18/10
(19' CLG)

MASTER
15/8 X 13/2
(9' CLG)

SPA

DESK
DN

PANTRY

DINING
10/8 X 14/2
(10' CLG)

FOYER

BUILT-IN

Copyright by designer/architect.
GARAGE
31/6 X 21/8

DEN
10/6 X 13/0
(9' CLG)

Images provided by designer/architect.

CAD FILE AVAILABLE

Basement Level

BR. 3
12/8 X 13/4
(9' CLG)

WET BAR

GAMES RM.
16/6 X 15/4
(9' CLG)

BR. 2
13/4 X 13/4
(9' CLG)

STORAGE

UP

LINEN

Rear Elevation

Plan #F01-441011

Dimensions: 67' W x 46' D
Levels: 1
Heated Square Footage: 2,898
Main Level Sq. Ft.: 1,743
Basement Level Sq. Ft.: 1,155
Bedrooms: 3
Bathrooms: 2½
Foundation: Walkout basement
Materials List Available: Yes
Price Category: F

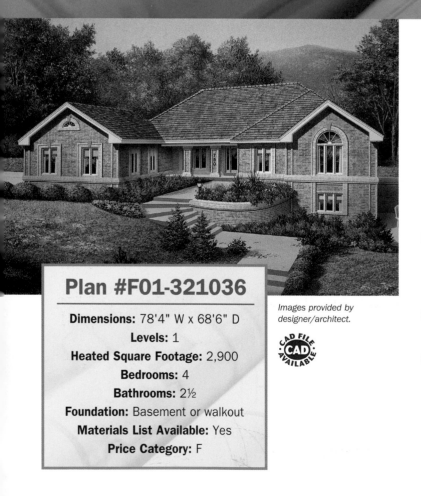

Plan #F01-321036

Dimensions: 78'4" W x 68'6" D
Levels: 1
Heated Square Footage: 2,900
Bedrooms: 4
Bathrooms: 2½
Foundation: Basement or walkout
Materials List Available: Yes
Price Category: F

Images provided by designer/architect.

CAD FILE AVAILABLE

Patio

Morning Rm
19-0x12-0

Great Rm
24-0x21-2
vaulted

MBr
16-0x17-5
coffered clg.

Kitchen
16-7x16-6

Dining
14-8x13-6
coffered clg.

Dn

Br 2
11-0x12-0

Entry

Br 4
12-10x14-9

Porch

Br 3
14-4x12-0

Garage
22-4x32-2

Copyright by designer/architect.

Wet Bar

Family
19-8x31-1

storage

Up

Br 5
14-4x12-0

Optional Basement

Copyright by designer/architect.

Images provided by designer/architect.

Bonus Area

Plan #F01-151845

Dimensions: 84'10" W x 69'4" D

Levels: 1

Heated Square Footage: 3,003

Bedrooms: 5

Bathrooms: 4

Foundation: Crawl space or slab; basement or walkout for fee

Materials List Available: No

Price Category: K

Copyright by designer/architect.

Images provided by designer/architect.

Plan #F01-151497

Dimensions: 74'2" W x 81'2" D

Levels: 1

Heated Square Footage: 3,021

Bedrooms: 4

Bathrooms: 3

Foundation: Slab

Materials List Available: No

Price Category: J

Images provided by designer/architect.

Plan #F01-171013

Dimensions: 74' W x 72' D

Levels: 1

Heated Square Footage: 3,084

Bedrooms: 4

Bathrooms: 3½

Foundation: Crawl space or slab

Materials List Available: Yes

Price Category: G

Impressive porch columns add to the country charm of this amenity-filled family home.

Features:

- Ceiling Height: 10 ft.

- Foyer: The sense of style continues from the front porch into this foyer, which opens to the formal dining room and the living room.

- Dining Room: Two handsome support columns accentuate the elegance of this dining room.

- Living Room: This living room features a cozy corner fireplace and plenty of room for the entire family to gather and relax.

- Kitchen: You'll be inspired to new culinary heights in this kitchen, which offers plenty of counter space, a snack bar, a built-in pantry, and a china closet.

- Master Suite: The bedroom of this master suite has a fireplace and overlooks a rear courtyard. The bath has two sinks, a large walk-in closet, a deluxe tub, a walk-in shower, and a skylight.

Plan #F01-541034

Dimensions: 79'6" W x 58'3"D
Levels: 1
Heated Square Footage: 3,162
Main Level Sq. Ft.: 2,113
Lower Level Sq. Ft.: 1,049
Bedrooms: 3
Bathrooms: 3
Foundation: Walkout; basement for fee
Materials List Available: No
Price Category: G

Images provided by designer/architect.

A combination of stone, shutters, and columns blend to create a magnificent exterior.

Features:

- Great Room: A see-through fireplace connects this vaulted gathering area to the kitchen and breakfast nook.

- Den: This den has built-in bookshelves and could serve as an additional bedroom.

- Master Suite: This fantastic suite features an octagon-shaped sitting area. The private bath includes a separate tub and shower, a walk-in closet, double sinks, and a vanity.

- Secondary Bedrooms: Located on the lower level, these two bedrooms share a Jack and Jill bathroom.

- Expansion: There is no lack of room to expand as the basement allows for a future sunken family room, another bedroom, and an additional bathroom.

Copyright by designer/architect.

Main Level

Lower Level

Plan #F01-161056

Dimensions: 86'2" W x 63'8" D
Levels: 1
Heated Square Footage: 3,171
Optional Lower Level Sq. Ft.: 1,897
Bedrooms: 3
Bathrooms: 2½
Foundation: Walkout; crawl space or basement for feee
Material List Available: Yes
Price Category: G

This home is dedicated to comfort and high lifestyle and sets the standard for excellence.

Images provided by designer/architect.

Features:

- **Open Plan:** A wraparound island with seating is adorned with pillars and arched openings, and it separates the kitchen from the great room and breakfast room. This design element allows the rooms to remain visually open and, paired with a 9-ft. ceiling height, creates a spacious area.

- **Great Room:** A gas fireplace warms this gathering area, and the wall of windows across the rear brings the outdoors in. The built-in entertainment center will be a hit with the entire family.

- **Master Suite:** Delighting you with its size and luxury, this retreat welcomes you with a double door entry and enjoys a stepped ceiling in the sleeping area. The master bath features a garden bathtub and an oversized walk-in closet.

- **Lower Level:** Open stairs introduce this lower level, which mimics the size of the first floor, and, with a 9-ft. ceiling height, offers the same elegant feel of the first floor. Additional bedrooms, game room, an exercise area, media room and storage are available options.

Optional Basement

Copyright by designer/architect.

Plan #F01-451321

Dimensions: 65' W x 56'6" D
Levels: 1
HeatedSquare Footage: 3,304
Main Level Sq. Ft.: 1,652
Lower Level Sq. Ft.: 1,652
Bedrooms: 2
Bathrooms: 3
Foundation: Slab or walkout
Materials List Available: No
Price Category: G

Images provided by designer/architect.

If you're searching for an ideal vacation home that's inviting and spacious enough to accommodate loved ones, this is it.

Features:

- Outdoor Living Space: With a covered porch and large open deck, sunbathers and barbecuers alike will enjoy relaxing outdoors.

- Kitchen: This room is perfect for relaxing or enjoying a home-cooked meal.

- Den: This den doubles as an office, or can be converted into an entertainment center for a movie night.

- Master Suite: This luxurious master suite features one of the three large bathrooms in the home.

- Garage: This two-car garage is ideal for multi-car families or those with a lot of sports equipment to store.

Rear Elevation

Copyright by designer/architect.

Copyright by designer/architect.

Family Rm. 17⁸ · 20⁰ 10'-0" Ceiling

Bath 3 7'-0" Ceiling

Covered Patio 10'-0" Ceiling

Nook 10'-0" Ceiling

Bedroom 4 12⁰ · 11⁴ 10'-0" Ceiling

Master Bedroom 15⁰ · 22⁰ 10'-0" Ceiling

Living Rm. 17⁰ · 18⁴ 12'-0" Ceiling

Kitchen 10'-0" Ceiling

Bedroom 3 12⁰ · 12⁰ 10'-0" Ceiling

w.i.c. w.i.c.

Bath 2 10'-0" Ceiling

Foyer

Dining Rm. 10¹⁰ · 15⁰ 10'-0" Ceiling

Bedroom 2 12⁴ · 12⁰ 10'-0" Ceiling

Den/Bdrm. 5 11¹ · 14⁹ 12'-0" Ceiling

M. Bath 10'-0" Ceiling

Entry

Laun.

3 Car Garage 27⁴ · 20⁰ 10' Ceiling

Plan #F01-661193

Dimensions: 64'8" W x 74'8" D

Levels: 1

Heated Square Footage: 3,060

Bedrooms: 4

Bathrooms: 3

Foundation: Slab

Materials List Available: No

Price Category: G

Images provided by designer/architect.

CAD FILE AVAILABLE

Copyright by designer/architect.

FAMILY ROOM 20'-0" X 23'-0" 12'-0" CLG.

COVERED PATIO 43'-3" X 18'-3" 12'-0" CLG.

SITTING 11'-11" WIDE 10'-0" CLG.

CAFE 9'-0" X 9'-0" 11'-0" CLG.

CABANA 6'-5" X 13'-0" 10'-0" CLG.

CLOSET

KITCHEN 13'-11" X 16'-2" 12'-0" CLG.

MASTER BEDROOM 18'-4" X 26'-0" 10'-0" to 10'-8" to 11'-4" CLG.

LIVING ROOM 16'-6" X 16'-2" 12'-0" to 13'-0" to 14'-0" CLG.

BEDROOM 2 13'-4" X 12'-0" 12'-0" CLG.

PAN.

BATH 13'-4" X 5'-6" 9'-0" CLG.

POWDER 5'-0" X 5'-6" 9'-0" CLG.

HIS W.I.C. 6' X 7'-4" 10' CLG.

HIS W.I.C. 5'X9'-10" 10' CLG.

CLOSET

MASTER BATH 14'-4" X 17'-10" 10'-0" CLG.

BEDROOM 3 12'-4" X 12'-6" 9'-0" CLG.

DINING 14'-10" X 12'-0" 11'-8" to 12'-4" CLG.

FOYER 7'-0" X 6'-8" 12'-0" CLG.

STUDY 12'-1" X 12'-0" 11'-8" to 12'-4" CLG.

CL.

LAUNDRY 10'-4" X 10'-8" 9'-0" CLG.

COVERED ENTRY 15'-8" X 12'-0" 14'-0" CLG.

CLOSET

2-CAR GARAGE 23'-0" X 20'-0" 9'-0" CLG.

DRIVEWAY

1-CAR GARAGE 20'-4" X 10'-8" 9'-0" CLG.

WORK AREA 15'-0" X 8'-11"

Plan #F01-611181

Dimensions: 78'2" W x 100' D

Levels: 1

Heated Square Footage: 3,455

Bedrooms: 3

Bathrooms: 2 Full, 2 Half

Foundation: Slab

Materials List Available: No

Price Category: G

Images provided by designer/architect.

CAD FILE AVAILABLE

Copyright by designer/architect.

Plan #F01-151060

Images provided by designer/architect.

CAD FILE AVAILABLE

Dimensions: 80'11" W x 95'8" D
Levels: 1
Heated Square Footage: 3,554
Bedrooms: 3
Bathrooms: 3
Foundation: Crawl space or slab; basement or walkout for fee
Materials List Available: Yes
Price Category: K

Copyright by designer/architect.

Optional Basement

Plan #F01-161028

Images provided by designer/architect.

Dimensions: 84'6" W x 69'4" D
Levels: 1
Heated Square Footage: 3,570
Opt. Finished Basement Sq. Ft.: 2,367
Bedrooms: 3
Bathrooms: 3½
Foundation: Basement
Materials List Available: No
Price Category: H

Plan #F01-161095

Dimensions: 59' W x 49'8" D
Levels: 1
Heated Square Footage: 3,620
Main Level Sq. Ft.: 2,068
Lower Level Sq. Ft.: 1,552
Bedrooms: 3
Bathrooms: 3
Foundation: Walkout; basement for fee
Materials List Available: No
Price Category: H

Images provided by designer/architect.

CAD FILE AVAILABLE

Main Level

Copyright by designer/architect.

Deck

Master Bedroom 15'-4" x 14'-0"

Breakfast 11'-0" x 13'-10"

Great Room 17'-9" x 16'-10"

Kitchen 15'-10" x 12'-10"

Home Office

Dressing

Bath

Laun.

Foyer

Dining Room 11'-8" X 13'-8"

Garage 22'-0" x 21'-0"

Bedroom Library 13'-0" x 14'-8"

Porch

Lower Level

Patio

Bedroom 14'-8" X 14'-8"

Bedroom 12'-0" X 12'-2"

Rec Room 22'-0" X 26'-0"

Bath

Hall

Bar

Basement

Billiards 13'-0" X 18'-6"

Unexcavated

Rear View

Plan #F01-481026

Dimensions: 72' W x 66' D
Levels: 1
Heated Square Footage: 3,837
Main Level Sq. Ft.: 2,374
Lower Level Sq. Ft.: 1,463
Bedrooms: 3
Bathrooms: 2½
Foundation: Walkout basement
Materials List Available: No
Price Category: H

Images provided by designer/architect.

Sitting 13-0 x 18-0 9' Clg

TV

Kit/Dinette 21-4 x 22-4 9' Clg

Great Rm 19-0 x 17-0 12' Clg

Master Suite 14-0 x 16-10 11' Tray Clg

FP

Built-In

DN

DW

Ref

WIC

D W

Folding

Bench

WIC

Dining 11-0 x 12-10 10' Raceway Clg

Foyer 12' Clg

Built-In

Copyright by designer/architect.

Garage 32-0 x 28-4

Study 11-0 x 12-4 10' Clg

Main Level

Rear Elevation

FP

UP

Mechanical

Family 23-0 x 20-0

Bedroom 2 14-0 x 13-10

Built-In

L

WIC

F

WH

Bedroom 3 13-10 x 13-10

WIC

Basement Level

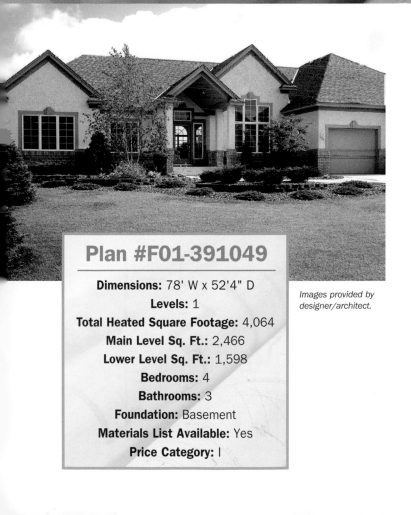

Images provided by designer/architect.

CAD FILE AVAILABLE

Plan #F01-211068

Dimensions: 98' W x 90' D

Levels: 1

Heated Square Footage: 3,960

Bedrooms: 4

Bathrooms: 4½

Foundation: Crawl space; basement or slab for fee

Materials List Available: Yes

Price Category: H

Images provided by designer/architect.

Plan #F01-391049

Dimensions: 78' W x 52'4" D

Levels: 1

Total Heated Square Footage: 4,064

Main Level Sq. Ft.: 2,466

Lower Level Sq. Ft.: 1,598

Bedrooms: 4

Bathrooms: 3

Foundation: Basement

Materials List Available: Yes

Price Category: I

Plan #F01-211067

Dimensions: 96' W x 90' D

Levels: 1

Heated Square Footage: 4,038

Bedrooms: 4

Bathrooms: 4½

Foundation: Crawl space; basement or slab for fee

Materials List Available: Yes

Price Category: I

Images provided by designer/architect.

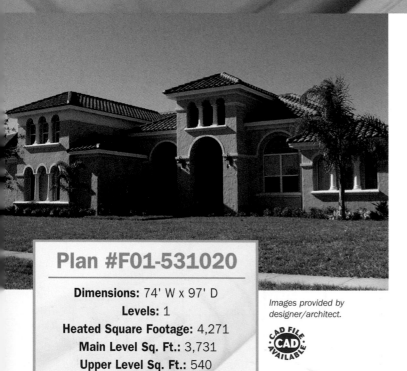

Plan #F01-531020

Dimensions: 74' W x 97' D

Levels: 1

Heated Square Footage: 4,271

Main Level Sq. Ft.: 3,731

Upper Level Sq. Ft.: 540

Bedrooms: 4

Bathrooms: 3½

Foundation: Slab

Materials List Available: No

Price Category: K

Images provided by designer/architect.

CAD FILE AVAILABLE

Copyright by designer/architect.

Main Level

Lower Level

Images provided by designer/architect.

CAD FILE AVAILABLE CAD

Plan #F01-451217

Dimensions: 103'6" W x 53'11" D
Levels: 1
Heated Square Footage: 4,711
Main Level Sq. Ft.: 2,470
Lower Level Sq. Ft.: 2,241
Bedrooms: 4
Bathrooms: 3
Foundation: Walkout basement
Materials List Available: No
Price Category: I

Main Level

Copyright by designer/architect.

Lower Level

Plan #F01-441212

Dimensions: 81' W x 66' D
Levels: 1
Heated Square Footage: 4,808
Main Level Sq. Ft.: 2,792
Lower Level Sq. Ft.: 2,016
Bedrooms: 4
Bathrooms: 4½
Foundation: Walkout
Materials List Available: Yes
Price Category: J

Images provided by designer/architect.

CAD FILE AVAILABLE CAD

Rear View

Plan #F01-481028

Dimensions: 86'8" W x 53' D
Levels: 1
Heated Square Footage: 3,980
Main Level Sq. Ft.: 2,290
Lower Level Sq. Ft.: 1,690
Bedrooms: 3
Bathrooms: 2½
Foundation: Walkout basement
Materials List Available: No
Price Category: H

Images provided by designer/architect.

• Master Suite: This romantic space features a 10-ft.-high stepped ceiling and a luxurious bath that includes a double-bowl vanity and a whirlpool tub.

• Lower Level: For fun times, this lower level is finished to provide a wet bar and a recreation room. Two bedrooms, which share a full bathroom, are also on this level. Future expansion can include an additional bedroom.

This home, with its Southwestern flair, invites friends and family in for some down-home hospitality.

Features:

• Foyer: A 12-ft-high ceiling extends an open welcome to all. With a view through the great room, the open floor plan makes the home feel large and open.

• Kitchen: This spacious gourmet kitchen opens generously to the hearth room, which features an angled fireplace. A two-level island, which contains a two-bowl sink, provides casual seating and additional storage.

Main Level

Lower Level

Rear View

Plan #F01-161093

Dimensions: 70'8" W x 64' D
Levels: 1
Heated Square Footage: 4,328
Main Level Sq. Ft.: 2,582
Lower Level Sq. Ft.: 1,746
Bedrooms: 3
Bathrooms: 3½
Foundation: Walkout
Materials List Available: No
Price Category: I

Detailed stucco and stone accents impart warmth and character to the exterior of this one level home.

Images provided by designer/architect.

Features:

- **Great Room:** This gathering room, which features a fireplace and a decorative ceiling, offers an extensive view of the rear yard.

- **Kitchen:** Spacious and up-to-date, this extra-large combination gourmet kitchen and breakfast room is an ideal area for doing chores and hosting family gatherings.

- **Main Level:** The extravagant master suite, with its private bathroom and dressing area, the library with built-in shelves, and the formal dining room round out the main floor. Accented by a wood rail, the extra-wide main stairway leads to the lavish lower level.

- **Lower Level:** The two additional bedrooms, adjoining bathroom, media room, billiard room, and exercise room comprise this fantastic finished lower level.

Great Room

Copyright by designer/architect.

Lower Level

Main Level

Plan #F01-441015

Dimensions: 130'3" W x 79'3" D
Levels: 1
Heated Square Footage: 4,732
Main Level Sq. Ft.: 2,902
Lower Level Sq. Ft.: 1,830
Bedrooms: 4
Bathrooms: 3 full, 2 half
Foundation: Walkout basement
Materials List Available: Yes
Price Category: J

CAD FILE AVAILABLE

Images provided by designer/architect.

An artful use of stone was employed on the exterior of this rustic hillside home to complement other architectural elements, such as the angled, oversize four-car garage and the substantial roofline.

Features:

• Great Room: This massive vaulted room features a large stone fireplace at one end and a formal dining area at the other. A built-in media center and double doors separate the great room from a home office with its own hearth and built-ins.

• Kitchen: This kitchen features a walk-in pantry and snack counter and opens to a skylighted outdoor kitchen. Its appointments include a cooktop and a corner fireplace.

• Home Theatre: This space has a built-in viewing screen, a fireplace, and terrace access.

• Lowe Level: Amazing resort-style living in the lower level of this home. It comes complete with 3 bedrooms, 2 baths, theater, full wet bar, wine cellar and plenty of unfinished space for storage.

Entry

• Master Suite: This private space is found at the other side of the home. Look closely for expansive his and her walk-in closets, a spa tub, a skylighted double vanity area, and a corner fireplace in the salon.

• Bedrooms: Three family bedrooms are on the lower level; bedroom 4 has a private bathroom and a walk-in closet.

• Garage: This large garage has room for four cars; don't miss the dog shower and grooming station just off the garage.

Great Room/Dining Area

Great Room

Outdoor Kitchen

Wet Bar

Study

Main Level

Lower Level

Why Buy Stock Plans?

Building a home from scratch presents many opportunities to showcase a homeowner's creativity, individuality, and dreams turned into reality.

Within these opportunities, many challenges and questions crop up. Location, size, and budget are all important to consider, as well as special features and amenities. When one really examines everything that must be determined, it can become overwhelming to search for your dream home. Before you get too anxious, start the search process with this question: Will you be using customized home plans or stock home plans?

Both types of home plan offer positives and negatives; what is "best" can only be determined by your lifestyle, budget, and time. A customized home plan is one that a homeowner and designer work together to develop from scratch, taking ideas and putting them down on paper. These plans are usually more expensive because you are starting from scratch and require extra patience, as it may be months before the architect has them ready. A stock plan is a pre-developed plan that fits the needs and desires of a group of people or general population. These are often available within days of purchasing and typically cost up to one-tenth the price of customized home plans.

When compared to a customizable plan, some homeowners fear that a stock home will produce carbon copy homes within a neighborhood, sapping the opportunities for individualism and creating a unique home. This is a common misconception that can waste a lot of money and time!

The variety of stock plans available is truly impressive, encompassing the most up-to-date features in square footage, room dimensions, layout, and amenities. With some patience and determination, sorting through the thousands of available stock plans can produce a dream home with plans that can be easily purchased and ready to go almost immediately. Most stock plans also have customizable options. For example, perhaps you see a stock plan that is just about perfect, but you wish the mudroom was a tad larger. Rather than go through the cost and time of having a customized design, you could submit a stock home plan modification (see page 281 for details) and have your new dream plans ready to go in no time. Also, the stock home plans have materials lists available, helping to eliminate unknown costs from developing during construction.

It's often a good idea to speak with someone who has recently built a home and learn from their experience. Did they use stock or customizable plans? What would they recommend you do or do not undertake? Can they recommend professionals that will help you narrow down your options?

Take the time to browse through home plan books making notes of questions or inquiries. Also take advantage of our website, **ultimateplans.com**. This website allows you to search for the perfect home plan by style, size, budget, and other particulars. With all these tools, you'll soon have the home plan of your dreams in your reality!

Modifying Your Plan

Have you found the almost perfect home but need to make a few changes to fit your needs? With Ultimate Plans that is not a problem. Beginning with a stock plan, our plan modification partner and their staff of designers can help you create the home of your DREAMS!

If you're like many customers, you may want to make changes to your home plan in order to make it the dream home you've always wanted. That's where our plan modification partner comes in. You won't find a more efficient and economic way to get your changes done.

Whether it's enlarging a kitchen, adding a porch or converting a crawl space to a basement, we can customize any plan and make it perfect for your family. Simply create your wish list and let us go to work. Soon you'll have the blueprints for your new home and at a fraction of the cost of hiring an architect!

The Ultimate Plans Modification Advantage

- We can customize any of the thousands of plans on ultimateplans.com.
- FREE cost estimates for your home plan modifications within 24-48 hours.
- Average turn-around time to complete the modifications is 2-3 weeks.
- One-on one design consultations.

Customizing Facts

- The average cost to customize a house plan is typically less than 1 percent of the building costs - compare that to the national average of 7 percent of building costs.
- The average modification cost for a home is typically $800 to $1,500 (this does not include the cost of the reproducible blueprint or PDF file, which is required to make plan changes).

Understanding The Process

We work with each customer/client individually to design your home. Once you have selected that primary design we will modify it to your personal needs.

After we understand your modification request, we will provide you with a custom quote for the stock plan purchase, architectural fees for the modifications and printing requirements.

When you decide to move forward with the plan purchase and your plan modifications, we will have a home plan modification proposal written up and emailed to you for your acceptance. All you need to do is fill in the needed information and send it back to us to get started.

When you purchase the primary plan and plan modifications, your home plan modification proposal will include the following:

1. Outline of the changes to be made
2. Number of copies to be provided
3. Timeline to provide the services
4. Cost to complete the design work
5. Other construction support services to consider.

Helpful tips to get you started on creating the home of your DREAMS!

Research the rules and regulations of the land or lot in which you intend to build. Are there restrictions such as building height, exterior finishes, easements, garage entrance, setbacks, or certain foundation types that can or cannot be built based on water tables?

Look ahead — Right now your family of three is perfectly comfortable in a two-bedroom house. However, what about a year or even five years from now? New additions to the family will need their own space, from children's nurseries to elderly parents who may move in with you. You cannot always perfectly anticipate your family's needs, but preparing now by finding a plan with an extra bathroom or a multifunctional bonus room is an excellent idea. In addition to space, look for plans that will allow easy incorporation of technological advances as well as good future resale value.

Know your weather—The weather not only affects the way you dress but also the way you outfit your home. New England homes have peaked roofs so heavy snow will fall off the roof rather than cave it in. Coastal homes that face tornado and hurricane assaults have flat roofs that help avoid detrimental wind damage. Be aware of what your dream home will need to avoid unnecessary work and repair in the future.

"Almost" does not cut it—The most important thing is to love the plan you choose and the modifications you incorporate. If something still does not seem right, do not ignore that feeling. Take the time to look the plan over carefully. Look at a few more stock plans and see if modifying a different plan would be better. Remember that modifications are being done to get exactly what you want, not just as-close-as possible.

Check with your local building department or builder in the area to find out what restrictions or codes need to be incorporated into you plan in order to obtain a building permit. Find out from your builder how many sets of plans they need.

Once you have determined the modifications you desire, it's time to get them done!

Visit www.ultimateplans.com to submit a free modification quote or CALL 1-866-441-2143

Home Plan Index— *for pricing see page 286*

Plan Number	Price Code	Page	Heated Square Feet	Material List	Plan Number	Price Code	Page	Heated Square Feet	Material List	Plan Number	Price Code	Page	Heated Square Feet	Material List
F01-101004	F	109	1787	Y	F01-151034	H	200	2133	N	F01-161073	D	124	1895	N
F01-101005	F	156	1992	Y	F01-151037	H	69	1538	N	F01-161079	B	51	1498	Y
F01-101006	F	154	1982	Y	F01-151039	F	30	1353	N	F01-161092	D	195	2110	Y
F01-101008	H	180	2088	Y	F01-151043	I	82	1636	N	F01-161093	I	277	4328	N
F01-101009	H	193	2097	Y	F01-151050	J	190	2096	N	F01-161095	H	272	3620	N
F01-101011	H	201	2184	Y	F01-151054	H	102	1746	N	F01-161115	E	210	2253	Y
F01-101012	H	218	2288	N	F01-151056	H	148	1950	N	F01-161196	E	233	2469	Y
F01-101013	H	250	2564	Y	F01-151057	K	261	2951	N	F01-161224	F	259	2796	Y
F01-101022	F	162	1992	Y	F01-151060	K	271	3554	Y	F01-161249	E	214	2246	Y
F01-101028	F	151	1963	N	F01-151068	I	128	1880	N	F01-171001	B	23	1277	N
F01-101030	F	175	2071	N	F01-151075	H	129	1909	N	F01-171004	E	211	2256	Y
F01-101033	H	215	2260	N	F01-151089	I	142	1921	N	F01-171006	C	84	1648	Y
F01-101169	H	168	2000	N	F01-151105	I	173	2039	N	F01-171008	C	85	1652	Y
F01-101177	F	149	1992	N	F01-151113	H	208	2186	N	F01-171009	C	103	1771	N
F01-111001	G	259	2832	Y	F01-151117	H	150	1957	N	F01-171013	G	266	3084	Y
F01-111004	G	262	2968	Y	F01-151138	H	165	2010	N	F01-171015	D	181	2089	Y
F01-111015	F	212	2208	Y	F01-151140	I	246	2525	N	F01-171023	C	88	1684	Y
F01-111017	F	219	2323	N	F01-151169	I	65	1525	N	F01-181021	E	15	1124	Y
F01-111018	G	257	2745	N	F01-151170	I	152	1965	N	F01-181148	E	13	1174	Y
F01-121001	D	133	1911	Y	F01-151171	I	199	2131	N	F01-181153	E	46	1478	Y
F01-121003	E	233	2498	Y	F01-151173	I	97	1739	N	F01-181159	G	155	1992	Y
F01-121008	C	84	1651	Y	F01-151188	I	242	2525	N	F01-181216	B	10	910	Y
F01-121009	B	40	1422	Y	F01-151196	H	115	1800	N	F01-181345	D	12	1079	Y
F01-121012	B	24	1195	Y	F01-151215	H	60	1519	N	F01-181708	I	260	2800	Y
F01-121034	E	212	2223	Y	F01-151233	H	127	1853	N	F01-181714	E	18	1244	Y
F01-121050	D	159	1996	Y	F01-151383	K	244	2534	N	F01-181727	G	30	1350	Y
F01-121053	E	231	2456	Y	F01-151463	H	71	1574	N	F01-191001	F	203	2156	N
F01-121116	E	216	2276	Y	F01-151486	I	247	2556	N	F01-191003	E	104	1785	N
F01-121117	D	203	2172	Y	F01-151495	H	196	2121	N	F01-191004	E	127	1856	N
F01-121118	C	93	1636	Y	F01-151497	J	265	3021	N	F01-191009	F	204	2172	N
F01-121121	C	29	1341	Y	F01-151529	F	44	1474	N	F01-191012	F	198	2123	N
F01-121144	B	16	1195	Y	F01-151594	I	258	2760	N	F01-191027	F	221	2354	N
F01-121163	F	252	2679	Y	F01-151598	H	146	1922	N	F01-191028	H	249	2669	N
F01-121331	G	103	1763	Y	F01-151608	H	72	1576	N	F01-191030	C	9	864	N
F01-131001	D	78	1615	Y	F01-151634	H	217	2285	N	F01-191032	F	181	2091	N
F01-131002	D	89	1709	Y	F01-151656	H	119	1806	N	F01-191037	E	72	1575	N
F01-131003	C	43	1466	N	F01-151703	J	194	2096	N	F01-191055	E	196	2123	N
F01-131005	D	75	1595	Y	F01-151802	I	249	2675	N	F01-191058	E	246	2550	N
F01-131007	D	73	1595	Y	F01-151842	I	197	2135	N	F01-211002	C	105	1792	Y
F01-131008	C	19	1299	Y	F01-151845	K	265	3003	N	F01-211005	D	161	2000	Y
F01-131010	D	80	1667	Y	F01-151850	J	192	2075	N	F01-211009	E	224	2396	Y
F01-131011	E	131	1897	Y	F01-151852	H	229	2424	Y	F01-211011	F	255	2791	Y
F01-131014	C	34	1380	N	F01-161001	C	108	1782	N	F01-211016	B	13	1191	Y
F01-131015	E	123	1860	Y	F01-161002	D	117	1860	Y	F01-211024	B	39	1418	Y
F01-131016	E	132	1902	Y	F01-161003	C	63	1508	Y	F01-211030	C	73	1600	Y
F01-131017	C	45	1480	Y	F01-161004	B	28	1315	Y	F01-211039	D	128	1868	Y
F01-131019	F	209	2243	Y	F01-161007	C	77	1611	Y	F01-211048	D	170	2002	Y
F01-131044	E	158	1994	Y	F01-161009	C	85	1651	N	F01-211049	D	166	2023	Y
F01-131045	F	220	2347	Y	F01-161010	C	67	1544	Y	F01-211059	E	218	2299	N
F01-131047	D	114	1793	Y	F01-161013	C	64	1509	N	F01-211062	F	253	2682	Y
F01-131052	E	223	2367	Y	F01-161014	C	94	1698	Y	F01-211067	I	274	4038	Y
F01-151002	J	227	2444	Y	F01-161026	D	178	2041	N	F01-211068	H	273	3960	Y
F01-151004	I	195	2107	Y	F01-161028	H	271	3570	N	F01-211151	E	220	2328	N
F01-151007	H	110	1787	N	F01-161037	E	232	2469	Y	F01-211155	F	256	2719	Y
F01-151009	H	99	1601	N	F01-161056	G	268	3171	Y	F01-221005	D	126	1851	N

Home Plan Index — *for pricing see page 286*

Plan Number	Price Code	Page	Heated Square Feet	Material List	Plan Number	Price Code	Page	Heated Square Feet	Material List	Plan Number	Price Code	Page	Heated Square Feet	Material List
F01-221009	C	118	1795	N	F01-341064	C	40	1418	Y	F01-401033	B	31	1405	Y
F01-221011	C	102	1756	N	F01-341128	B	38	1410	Y	F01-401047	B	12	1064	Y
F01-221013	B	47	1495	N	F01-341146	A	11	960	N	F01-421009	F	248	2649	Y
F01-221015	D	143	1926	N	F01-341304	C	18	1248	Y	F01-431001	C	113	1792	Y
F01-221016	B	42	1461	N	F01-351001	H	122	1855	Y	F01-441001	E	121	1850	N
F01-221018	D	170	2007	N	F01-351002	H	100	1751	Y	F01-441002	E	125	1873	N
F01-221099	D	120	1829	Y	F01-351003	H	106	1751	Y	F01-441003	E	74	1580	N
F01-241001	E	222	2350	N	F01-351004	H	126	1852	Y	F01-441004	E	96	1728	N
F01-241005	C	81	1670	N	F01-351005	H	62	1501	N	F01-441005	E	116	1800	N
F01-241007	D	171	2036	N	F01-351006	H	83	1638	Y	F01-441006	E	130	1891	N
F01-241008	E	243	2526	N	F01-351007	H	214	2251	Y	F01-441008	F	169	2001	N
F01-241017	E	230	2431	N	F01-351008	H	167	2002	Y	F01-441009	G	251	2650	Y
F01-241041	C	82	1612	N	F01-351009	F	37	1400	N	F01-441010	G	263	2973	Y
F01-251001	B	21	1253	Y	F01-351020	F	48	1488	Y	F01-441011	F	264	2898	Y
F01-251003	B	33	1393	Y	F01-351023	H	76	1600	Y	F01-441015	J	278	4732	Y
F01-251004	C	70	1550	Y	F01-351033	H	79	1654	Y	F01-441055	E	116	1800	N
F01-251006	D	121	1849	Y	F01-351038	H	119	1800	Y	F01-441212	J	275	4808	Y
F01-271005	B	31	1368	Y	F01-351047	H	164	2001	Y	F01-451217	I	275	4711	N
F01-271007	B	25	1283	Y	F01-351053	I	194	2100	Y	F01-451321	G	269	3304	N
F01-271073	D	145	1920	N	F01-351062	H	62	1502	Y	F01-481026	H	272	3837	N
F01-271074	E	228	2400	N	F01-351069	H	171	2008	Y	F01-481028	H	276	3980	N
F01-271076	D	205	2188	N	F01-351071	H	202	1600	Y	F01-481154	D	146	1918	N
F01-271077	C	104	1786	N	F01-351088	H	232	2500	Y	F01-501549	C	63	1502	Y
F01-271079	E	213	2228	N	F01-351102	I	169	2000	Y	F01-501723	D	197	2125	N
F01-271081	E	245	2539	N	F01-351105	I	176	2000	Y	F01-531020	K	274	4271	N
F01-271082	D	179	2074	N	F01-351126	H	178	2021	Y	F01-541034	G	267	3162	N
F01-281022	C	61	1506	Y	F01-351146	H	68	1509	Y	F01-561005	E	226	2358	N
F01-281031	B	47	1493	Y	F01-351186	H	147	1924	Y	F01-611110	F	258	2762	N
F01-291001	C	70	1550	N	F01-351203	H	230	2447	Y	F01-611181	G	270	3455	N
F01-301005	D	144	1930	Y	F01-351205	H	147	1934	Y	F01-661004	E	228	2397	N
F01-321001	E	90	1721	Y	F01-351206	H	202	2140	Y	F01-661007	F	248	2660	N
F01-321002	D	36	1400	Y	F01-371007	D	148	1944	N	F01-661073	D	179	2041	N
F01-321003	E	111	1791	Y	F01-371011	C	92	1681	N	F01-661160	F	215	2258	N
F01-321007	G	256	2695	Y	F01-371030	B	41	1434	N	F01-661193	G	270	3060	N
F01-321008	C	98	1761	Y	F01-371033	C	91	1724	N	F01-761001	B	207	2025	Y
F01-321009	E	92	1684	Y	F01-371042	D	160	1999	N	F01-761002	C	180	2241	Y
F01-321010	C	105	1787	Y	F01-371049	B	41	1440	N	F01-761004	E	153	2241	Y
F01-321013	B	32	1360	Y	F01-371059	E	213	2240	N	F01-761005	B	8	1281	Y
F01-321019	E	231	2452	Y	F01-371093	B	19	1300	N	F01-761006	C	229	1582	Y
F01-321026	C	94	1712	Y	F01-371095	F	257	2725	N	F01-761008	C	120	1562	Y
F01-321027	F	254	2758	Y	F01-371104	C	118	1795	N	F01-761009	C	86	1762	Y
F01-321030	F	172	2029	Y	F01-381010	E	129	1905	Y	F01-761012	D	87	1820	Y
F01-321033	D	22	1268	Y	F01-391008	B	27	1312	Y	F01-761013	C	216	1562	Y
F01-321036	F	264	2900	Y	F01-391019	C	112	1792	N	F01-761014	E	217	2487	Y
F01-321037	F	225	2397	Y	F01-391021	C	71	1568	Y	F01-761019	F	247	2814	Y
F01-321224	C	68	1519	Y	F01-391034	C	95	1737	Y	F01-761031	D	221	2156	Y
F01-321330	B	39	1414	Y	F01-391038	C	83	1642	Y	F01-761039	C	149	1624	Y
F01-321371	E	219	2305	Y	F01-391039	C	69	1539	Y	F01-761045	C	93	2050	Y
F01-341004	C	14	1101	Y	F01-391049	I	273	4064	Y	F01-761047	D	174	1983	Y
F01-341023	C	46	1469	Y	F01-391138	D	206	2194	Y	F01-761048	B	49	1615	Y
F01-341026	B	11	1009	Y	F01-401008	C	66	1541	Y	F01-761049	C	168	2100	Y
F01-341028	C	20	1248	Y	F01-401020	B	17	1230	Y					
F01-341029	C	95	1737	Y	F01-401022	B	50	1495	Y					
F01-341030	C	86	1660	Y	F01-401024	B	26	1298	Y					
F01-341035	C	87	1680	Y	F01-401025	B	38	1408	Y					

Included in Our Plan Packages

"Square footage" refers to the total "heated square feet" of the plan. This number does not include the garage, porches, or unfinished bonus areas. All of our home plans are the result of many hours of work by leading architects and professional designers.

Below is a sample of the plan information included for most of the designs in this book. Specific details may vary with each designer's plan. While this information is typical of most plans, we cannot assure the inclusion of all the following referenced items. Please contact our customer service department for plan specific information, including which of the following items are included.

Front Cover Sheet

Many plans include the artist's rendering of the front of the house. It gives you an idea of how the house will look once it is completed and the property landscaped.

Detailed Floor Plans

These plans show the size and layout of the rooms. They also provide the locations of doors, windows, fireplaces, closets, stairs, and electrical outlets and switches.

Foundation Plan

A foundation plan gives the dimensions of basements, walk-out basements, crawl spaces, pier foundations, and slab construction. Each house design lists the type of foundation included. If the plan you choose does not have the foundation type you require, our customer service department can help you customize the plan to meet your needs.

Roof Plan

In addition to providing the pitch of the roof, some plans also show the locations of dormers, skylights, and other elements.

Exterior Elevations

These drawings show the front, rear, and sides of the house as if you were looking at it head on. Elevations also provide information about architectural features and finish materials.

Interior Elevations and Details

Interior elevations show specific details of such elements as fireplaces, kitchen and bathroom cabinets, built-ins, and other unique features of the design.

Cross Section

This shows the structure as if it were sliced to reveal construction requirements, such as insulation, flooring, and roofing details.

Illustrations provided by designer/architect

Decide What Type of Plan Package You Need

How Many Plans Should You Order?

Standard 8-Set Package. We've found that our 8-set package is the best value for someone who is ready to start building. The 8-set package provides plans for you, your builder, the subcontractors, mortgage lender, and the building department.

Minimum 5-Set Package. If you are in the bidding process, you may want to order only five sets for the bidding round and reorder additional sets as needed.

1-Set Study Package. We offer a 1-set study package so you can review your home in great detail. This one set is considered a study set and is marked "not for construction." It is a copyright violation to reproduce blueprints. This plan cannot be exchanged or returned, it can only be upgraded to a full build set of the same plan.

Buying Additional Sets. If you require additional copies of blueprints for your home construction, you can order additional sets within 90 days of the original order date at a reduced price. The cost is $45.00 for each additional set. For more information, contact our customer service department.

Note: All plan packages listed on order form are not available for every plan. Plan packages vary by plan. Check our website for availability.

Mirror-Reverse/Right-Reading Reverse

Plans can be printed in mirror-reverse — we can "flip" plans to create a mirror image of the design. This is useful when the house would fit your site or personal preferences if all the rooms were on the opposite side than shown. As the image is reversed, the lettering and dimensions will also be reversed, meaning they will read backwards. Therefore, when ordering mirror-reverse drawings, you must order at least one set of the original plan unreversed. A $15.00 fee per plan will be charged for mirror-reverse (regardless of the number of mirror-reverse sets ordered). Some plans are available in right-reading reverse; this feature will show the plan in reverse, but the writing on the plan will be readable. A $150.00 fee per plan order will be charged for right-reading reverse. Please contact our customer service department or visit, ultimateplans.com to check the availability of this feature for your chosen plan.

CAD (Computer-Aided Design) Files

A CAD package is a complete set of construction drawings in an electronic file format. They are especially beneficial if you have a significant amount of changes to make to the home plan you have selected, or if you need to make the home plan fit your local codes. If you purchase a CAD Package, you have the option to take the plan to a local design professional who uses AutoCAD or DataCAD and they can modify the design much easier and quicker than with a paper-based drawing, which will help save you time and money. Just like our reproducible masters, with a CAD package you will receive a one-time build copyright release that allows you to make changes and the necessary copies needed to build your home. For more information and availability, please call our Customer Service Department at 1-800-523-6789.

Note: CAD files are non-refundable and not returnable.

Reproducible Masters

If you wish to make some minor design changes, you'll want to order reproducible masters. These drawings contain the same information as the blueprints, but are printed on reproducible paper and clearly indicate your right to alter, copy or reproduce. This will allow your builder or a local design professional to make the necessary drawing changes without the major expense of redrawing the plans. This package also allows you to print copies of the modified plans as needed. The right of building only one structure from these plans is licensed exclusively to the buyer. You may not use this design to build a second or multiple dwelling(s) without purchasing another blueprint. Each violation of the Copyright Law is punishable in a fine.

Note: Once package is opened, reproducible masters are not returnable.

PDF Files

This option is a complete set of construction drawings in an electronic format that allows you to resize and reproduce the plans to fit your needs. Since these are electronic files, we can send them to you within 24 hours (Mon-Fri, 7:30 - 4:30 CST) via email and save you shipping costs. They also offer printing flexibility by allowing you to print the size and number of sets you need. Note: These are not CAD files and cannot be altered electronically.
Note: PDF files are non-refundable and not returnable.

EZ Quote® : Home Cost Estimator

EZ Quote® is our response to a frequently asked question from customers: "How much will the house cost me to build?" EZ Quote®: Home Cost Estimator will enable you to obtain a calculated building cost to construct your home, based on labor rates and building material costs within your zip code area. This summary is useful for those who want to get an idea of the total construction costs before purchasing sets of home plans. It will also provide a level of comfort when you begin soliciting bids. The cost is $29.95 for the first EZ Quote® and $19.95 for each additional one in the same order. Available only in the U.S. and Canada.

Materials List

Available for most of the plans in this book, the materials list gives you the quantity, dimensions and description of the building materials necessary to construct your home. The material list is intended to be used only in conjunction with the corresponding blueprints and specifications, and is not intended to be used solely for ordering purposes. Extreme care has gone into assuring that your material lists is accurate. However, due to variations in local building practices and widely differing code requirements, the exact material quantities cannot be guaranteed. See the Home Plan Index on pages 282-283 for availability.

Note: Material lists are designed with the standard foundations only and will not include alternate or optional foundations. Please review the material list and the construction drawings with your builder and material supplier in order to verify product line, color, measurements, and descriptions of the materials listed.

Before You Order

Exchange Policies

Since blueprints are printed in response to your order, we cannot honor requests for refunds. However, if for some reason you find that the plan you have purchased does not meet your requirements, you may exchange that plan for another plan in our collection within 90 days of purchase. At the time of the exchange, you will be charged a processing fee of 25% of your original plan package price, plus the difference in price between the plan packages (if applicable) and the cost to ship the new plans to you.

Note: Reproducible masters can only be exchanged if the package is unopened. PDF files and CAD packages are not returnable and non-refundable.

Building Codes & Requirements

At the time the construction drawings were prepared, every effort was made to ensure that these plans and specifications meet nationally recognized codes. Because building codes vary from area to area, some drawing modifications and/or the assistance of a professional designer or architect may be necessary to comply with your local codes or to accommodate specific building site conditions. We advise you to consult with your local building official for information regarding codes governing your area.

Blueprint Price Schedule

Price Code	1 Set	5 Sets	8 Sets	Repro Masters or PDF Files	CAD	Materials List
A	$430	$530	$630	$730	$1,180	$125
B	$490	$590	$690	$790	$1,375	$125
C	$550	$650	$750	$850	$1,550	$125
D	$600	$700	$800	$900	$1,655	$125
E	$650	$750	$850	$950	$1,760	$125
F	$725	$825	$925	$1,025	$1,890	$125
G	$760	$860	$960	$1,060	$1,940	$125
H	$780	$880	$980	$1,080	$1,995	$125
I	$1,045	$1,145	$1,245	$1,345	$2,215	$125
J	$1,250	$1,350	$1,450	$1,550	$2,415	$125
K	$1,255	$1,355	$1,455	$1,555	$2,415	$125
L	$1,300	$1,400	$1,500	$1,600	$2,520	$125

Note: All prices subject to change without notice.
Please note that plans and material lists are not refundable.

Shipping & Handling   Alaska and Hawaii US Express Only

US Regular (7–10 business days) $25	**Canada Standard** (8–12 business days) $45
US Priority (3–5 business days) $45	**Canada Express** (3–5 business days) $100
US Express (1–2 business days) $60	
Worldwide Express (3–5 business days) ** Quote Required **	

Note: Shipping and handling does not apply for PDF files.
Orders will be emailed within 24 hours of purchase—(Monday–Friday CST).

License To Build

When you purchase a "full set of construction drawings" from Design America, Inc., you are purchasing an exclusive one-time "License to Build," not the rights to the design. Design America, Inc. is granting you permission on behalf of the home plan designer to use the construction drawings one time for the building of your dream home. The construction drawings (also referred to as blueprints/plans and any derivative of that plan whether extensive or minor) are still owned and protected under copyright laws by the original designer. The blueprints/plans cannot be resold, transferred, rented, loaned or used by anyone other than the original purchaser of the "License to Build" without written consent from Design America, Inc. or the home plan designer.
Note: A "full set of construction drawings" consist of a (5) or (8) set plan package, a reproducible master, a PDF file, or a CAD package.

Multiple Plan Discount

Purchase 3 different home plans in the same order and receive 5% off the plan price. Purchase 5 or more different home plans in the same order and receive 10% off the plan price.
Note: Study sets do not apply.

Note: All plan packages listed on order form are not available for every plan. Plan packages vary by plan.
Check our website for availability.

Order Form

Please send me the following:

Plan Number: F01-_____

Price Code:_____ *(See Plan Index.)*

Indicate Foundation Type: (Select ONE. See plan page for availability.)

❏ Slab ❏ Crawl space ❏ Basement

❏ Walk-out basement ❏ Pier

❏ Optional Foundation for Fee of $250

Enter foundation type here_____ $ _____
  * Please call all our customer service department,
    or visit our website ultimateplans.com for availability

Basic Blueprint Package   Cost

❏ CAD Files *(call for availability)* $ _____

❏ PDF Files *(call for availability)* $ _____

❏ Reproducible Masters $ _____

❏ 8-Set Plan Package $ _____

❏ 5-Set Plan Package $ _____

❏ 1-Set Study Package *(no mirror reverse)* $ _____

❏ Additional plan sets*:
    _____ sets at $45.00 per set $ _____

❏ Print in mirror-reverse: $15.00 per plan $ _____
    * Where right reading is not available

❏ Print in right-reading reverse: $150.00 fee $ _____
    * Please call all our customer service department,
      or visit our website ultimateplans.com for availability

Important Extras

❏ Materials List* starting at $125 *(see index)* $ _____

❏ EZ Quote® for Plan #_____at $29.95 $ _____

❏ Additional EZ Quotes for Plan #s_____ $ _____

    Plan #_____at $19.95 each

Shipping (see page 286) $ _____

SUBTOTAL $ _____

Sales Tax (MO residents only, add 8.425%) $ _____

TOTAL $ _____

*Available only within 90 days after purchase of plan.

Name _____
(Please print or type)

Street _____
(Please do not use a P.O. Box)

City _____ State _____

Country _____ Zip _____

Daytime telephone (_____) _____

E-Mail _____

Payment ❏ Bank check/money order. No personal checks.
Make checks payable to Design America, Inc.

❏ VISA ❏ MasterCard ❏ AMERICAN EXPRESS Cards ❏ DISCOVER

Credit card number _____

Expiration date (mm/yy) _____ CID _____

Signature _____

❏ *I hereby authorize Design America, Inc. to charge this*
   purchase to my credit card.

Please check the appropriate box:

❏ Building home for myself

❏ Building home for someone else

ORDER ONLINE
ultimateplans.com

Order Toll Free by Phone
1-800-523-6789
By Fax: 314-770-2226

Order Online
www.ultimateplans.com

Express Delivery
Most orders are processed within
24 hours of receipt. If you need to place
a rush order, please call us by 11:00 a.m.
Monday through Friday and ask for express
service. Home plan representatives are
available from 7:30 a.m.–4:30 p.m. CST.

Mail Your Order
Design America, Inc.
Attn: Ultimate Plan Order
734 West Port Plaza, Suite #208
St. Louis, MO 63146

Canadian Customers
Order Toll Free 1-800-393-1883

Copyright Notice